APOCALYPTIC

APOCALYPTIC

LEON MORRIS

WM. B. EERDMANS PUBLISHING CO.

First printing, July 1972
Fourth printing, December 1980

CONTENTS

PREFACE

This little book is not meant to be a profound or original contribution to a difficult subject. It is written out of two convictions: the one, that apocalyptic is an important part of the background of the New Testament, the other, that it is not well understood by the average student. Indeed, I fear that the average student would be hard put to it to give more than one or two characteristics of this kind of literature. I have written accordingly to help him get the picture. Recognizing that experts in apocalyptic differ widely among themselves and that there are many points of uncertainty, I have tried to show what are the generally held opinions and what are the controverted areas. This then is simply an introduction to a very important but little understood part of the background of the New Testament.

In writing it I have learned much from those who have worked at the difficult problems posed by this literature. I have tried to indicate my indebtedness with acknowledgments in the footnotes.

LEON MORRIS

PREFACE TO THE SECOND EDITION

Some readers of the first edition of this little study suggested that it would have been more useful had some treatment of Old Testament apocalyptic been included. Though the book was intended primarily as a study of the background of New Testament apocalyptic there seems no reason why attention should not be given to the Old Testament as well. The main treatment of the subject is as applicable to the one Testament as to the other. So in this second edition I have included a section on the Old Testament. Apart from this changes have been minor. I have reworded one or two places to make the meaning clearer and have included a few more references.

One reviewer of the first edition took the line that the book was a discussion of the statement of Käsemann with which it opens. So perhaps I should make it clear that the book is nothing of the sort. For that a very different approach would be needed. Käsemann's words are no more than a jumping-off point. The book is meant as a summary of the characteristics of apocalyptic.

LEON MORRIS

INTRODUCTION

'Apocalyptic – since the preaching of Jesus cannot really be described as theology – was the mother of all Christian theology.'[1] So writes E. Käsemann. His statement is perhaps extreme, but it expresses the mood of a good deal of writing today. Many are excited at the new possibilities that open up before us as we see the New Testament against an apocalyptic background. D. N. Freedman expresses much the same confident spirit as Käsemann when he speaks of the 'discovery and subsequent demonstration that the controlling factor in the literature of the New Testament is apocalyptic'.[2] Käsemann sees apocalyptic as the 'mother' of Christian theology, Freedman as the 'controlling factor' in New Testament literature. Both ascribe to it a dominating role.

Others reach much the same position through a consideration of leading New Testament concepts. Ethelbert Stauffer did this some time back when he described 'the Kingdom of God' and 'the Son of Man' as technical terms in apocalyptic. He went on to maintain that the crucial problems dealt with by the New Testament writers are all subjects that have previously been the concern of the apocalyptists. He sums up: 'In fine, the NT writers are rooted, so far as their exegetical and theological thought forms go, in a living tradition which comes to them from the OT via the apocryphal literature down to the apocalyptic national writings of their own time.'[3] If this is the case, then clearly we must become familiar with

[1] E. Käsemann, in *Journal for Theology and the Church*, no. 6, 1969, p. 40. R. H. Charles similarly speaks of apocalyptic as 'the parent of Christianity' (*The Apocrypha and Pseudepigrapha of the Old Testament*, ii, Oxford, 1963, p. 1).

[2] D. N. Freedman, in *Journal for Theology and the Church*, no. 6, 1969, p. 167.

[3] E. Stauffer, *New Testament Theology*, London, 1955, p. 20.

apocalyptic if we are to understand what the New Testament
writers are saying. William A. Beardslee points to this when
he says, 'Many of the central New Testament symbols for
interpreting God's coming to man, including the resurrection, the Kingdom of God, and the Messiah or Christ, are
apocalyptic symbols.'[4] Notice that among the concepts he
selects are some that students of the New Testament have
usually thought could safely be interpreted without recourse
to apocalyptic. If concepts that we have hitherto understood
apart from apocalyptic are now shown in fact to be apocalyptic terms, then we must think again about a great deal of
our exegesis of the New Testament.

It is this that makes the subject so important right now.
I do not mean to infer that we must necessarily agree with
writers such as those cited. We shall presently notice a different opinion. But whether we agree with them or not, we
must know something about apocalyptic. Otherwise we shall
not know whether we are meeting it or not. It is plain that
apocalyptic ideas were more widely held in New Testament
times than has always been realized. Nobody denies that this
type of thinking is behind some at any rate of the New Testament. So study of this kind of writing is more than ever
necessary.

But it would be wrong to give the impression that all or
even most scholars unhesitatingly accept apocalyptic as the
key that will unlock all the mysteries of the New Testament.
Some oppose such an idea with considerable vigour. Wayne
G. Rollins, for example, has written a very incisive article
in which he takes issue with Käsemann and his allies.[5] Rollins
refuses to see apocalyptic as anything more than one strand
in a very complex pattern. And it is not an original strand.
That is to say, he flatly denies Käsemann's contention that it
was 'the mother of all Christian theology'. Other theological
ideas were found in the early church, he thinks, before
apocalyptic gained entrance. He also finds certain aspects of
early Christianity opposed to the main thrust of apocalyptic.

[4] W. A. Beardslee, in *Interpretation*, xxv, 1971, p. 419.
[5] W. G. Rollins, 'The New Testament and Apocalyptic', in *New
Testament Studies*, 17, 1970–71, pp. 454–476.

For example, the church was incurably interested in Christology, and Christology 'was inextricably rooted in the life-teaching-death-resurrection of Jesus of Nazareth'.[6] In other words, the church looked back to Jesus; apocalyptic looked forward to the End. Of course the church also looked for the End, but not in the same way as did apocalyptic. For the apocalyptist the whole of history pointed to the End and he concentrated his gaze on it. But the church saw the End as the consummation of what God had already begun in sending His Son. While not minimizing the significance of the parousia, it was the incarnation that was critically important. Rollins also notices that, whereas apocalyptic sees history as meaningless, the church saw God's word as already producing results within history. God discloses Himself in history. The present world has meaning for Christianity that it lacks for apocalyptic. He thinks also that the Christians put more emphasis on preaching and less on the written word than did the apocalyptists.

Criticisms like these are serious and must be given due weight. They make it difficult to see New Testament Christianity as fundamentally apocalyptic in character. If any position like that of Käsemann is to be maintained they must be answered. There appears to be an interesting battle ahead as New Testament scholars grapple with these opposing points of view. But whatever the ultimate outcome, I do not see how it can be denied that apocalyptic was one strand in the fabric of early church teaching (as Rollins himself allows). We must have some understanding of it.

It has, of course, been plain for a long time that we need some understanding of apocalyptic if we are to read our New Testaments intelligently. To cite nothing else, one reason for the widespread neglect of the book of Revelation by many ordinary Christians, and also for its eager misinterpretation among certain ardent students of prophecy, is that modern Christians in general simply do not know what to make of this kind of literature. We no longer write it (at least in its biblical form; there are some modern writers who employ an apocalyptic style and who may not unfairly be designated

[6] *Ibid.*, p. 472.

'apocalyptists'; but for all their resemblance to the classical apocalyptists they are not writing in the same genre). We have lost the clue to its meaning. Thus a determined effort must be made if we are to make sense of Revelation. The same, of course, applies to the expressions derived from this type of literature in the Gospels and in other parts of the New Testament (*e.g.* 2 Thes. 2).

FIRST-CENTURY JUDAISM

There are obvious differences between Christianity and what has been called 'normative Judaism', the form in which Judaism with its distinctive tenets finally emerged. This is usually understood to have been a development of the Pharisaic position,[1] and the Pharisees appear in the Gospels as determined opponents of Jesus and His followers. These differences make it difficult to think of the Christian movement as having evolved from Pharisaism, though some have thought this to have been the case.[2] It is much more likely that it found its adherents among the followers of one or more of the other ways of life that existed among the Jews of the time. We have always known that there were other Jewish groups, such as the Sadducees, the Herodians and the Essenes. We have known little about them, for their writings have not been preserved. But enough has been known for it to be fairly clear that we are to locate the Christian movement in some such circles rather than see it as a development of Pharisaism.

Some of these other Jewish groups were characterized by 'enthusiasm'. That is to say, they put a good deal of emphasis on new revelations and the like. They expected God to be active in the affairs of men and looked for evidence of this activity in their own circles. They stressed immediate

[1] W. D. Davies, however, cautions us against following Josephus in exaggerating the importance of the Pharisees in New Testament times (*Peake's Commentary on the Bible*, ed. M. Black and H. H. Rowley, London, 1962, p. 705). But his point is rather that the importance of people like the zealots has been underestimated than that the Pharisaic position did not triumph eventually.

[2] For example P. Winter says, '. . . *in historical reality Jesus was a Pharisee. His teaching was Pharisaic teaching*' (*On the Trial of Jesus*, Berlin, 1961, p. 133; Winter's italics). But the arguments brought against this seem decisive. See, for example, D. R. Catchpole in *The Trial of Jesus*, ed. E. Bammel, London, 1970, pp. 48–51.

religious experience and the workings of the Spirit of God. Their religion was not as formal as that of the chief priests or the Sadducees or the Pharisees. It included a marked element of spontaneity. While they had great respect for the Law, they did not look at it in quite the same way as did the Pharisees. They had a more dynamic understanding of revelation, where it would not be unfair to suggest that the Pharisees saw it as static, at least by comparison. The Pharisees stressed the 'given' element in the Law. The Law, it is true, could be thought about and expounded in such a way as to bring out new applications and new understandings in new situations. But the idea that God had made a fresh revelation, something not in the Law, came from a different world. It was quite foreign to the Pharisees.

But it was not foreign to all the Jews around the turn of our era. That God had made other revelations, some of them having been made, or at least having become known, only quite recently, was accepted by not a few enthusiasts. This was heady stuff and it is not surprising that some Jews of the time had a very different understanding of God's ways from that which was characteristic of the establishment.

It is with this side of Judaism that Christianity must be connected. It seems impossible to understand it as a development of the more formal and official type of Jewish religion. Its original adherents must have come largely from this 'enthusiastic' section of the nation. What Käsemann and his allies are suggesting is that we should not look to 'enthusiastic' circles generally and say no more than that it was from somewhere in this general region that Christianity emerged. They are saying that we can speak specifically of apocalypticism as the matrix for Christian theology.

Perhaps this is the place where we should notice the relations between Pharisaism and apocalypticism. The subject is one of great difficulty and the most varied opinions have been held. Thus George Foot Moore thought of the Pharisees and of the Judaism that developed from them as completely out of sympathy with apocalyptic. He saw it as 'a fallacy of method for the historian to make them [the apocalypses] a primary source for the eschatology of Judaism, much more to contaminate its theology with them'.[3] He thought of the Gospels and the early part of Acts as 'witnesses to authentic Jewish tradition, while the apocalypses (and the kindred element in the Gospels) represent groups, or at least tendencies, outside the main current of thought and life'.[4] On the other hand, C. C. Torrey could say, 'The Jewish apocalyptic writings were not the property of any sect or school. Their point of view was in general that of Palestinian orthodoxy, of the type of which the Pharisees were the best representatives.'[5] More recently the new edition of the Hastings one-volume *Dictionary of the Bible* has taken much the same line. The apocalypses, it says, 'are the output of one phase of Pharisaism, which while elevating both Torah and the Oral Law was not content with bald legalism, but dared trust in the realization of its religious hopes'.[6] It is not easy to see how such diverse views can be reconciled or to see where the evidence is that may afford us the means of judging between them. The problem is the paucity of literature from the New Testament period setting forth the Pharisaic position. The great Jewish collections, the Mishnah, the Talmud and others, are much later, and, while everybody agrees that they embody a great deal of early material, it is not easy to identify enough of it that is relevant for us to decide such an issue.

Perhaps the best view until further evidence comes to light is that which recognizes some change within Jewish orthodoxy. While some apocalyptic concepts still remain in the later Rabbinic literature, there can be no doubt but that as a whole it is antagonistic to all that apocalyptic stands for. But there seems no reason for holding that this was the earliest state of affairs. R. H. Charles held that in pre-Christian times 'apocalyptic Judaism' and 'legalistic Judaism' were not essen-

---

[3] G. F. Moore, *Judaism*, i, Harvard, 1958, p. 127. He also says of the apocalypses, '. . . not only are the writings themselves ignored in the Tannaite literature, but many of the subjects with which they deal are foreign to it' (*ibid.*).

[4] *Ibid.*, p. 132.

[5] C. C. Torrey, in *The Jewish Encyclopedia*, i, p. 673.

[6] *Dictionary of the Bible*, 2nd ed., orig. ed. by James Hastings, rev. F. C. Grant and H. H. Rowley, Edinburgh, 1963, p. 821.

tially antagonistic. But he thinks that in time the apocalyptic
wing of Judaism passed over to Christianity. He sees the
destruction of the temple as a significant happening: 'Before
AD 70 Judaism was a Church with many parties: after AD 70
the legalistic party succeeded in suppressing its rivals.'[7] W. D.
Davies is another who sees some kinship between Pharisaism
and apocalyptic. He adduces considerations which 'at least
invalidate any complete differentiation of Apocalyptic from
Pharisaism'.[8] Again he says, 'To deny the difference of
emphasis in Apocalyptic and Pharisaism would be idle, but
it is grievously erroneous to enlarge this difference into a
cleavage.'[9]

A different but important question is the relationship of
Jesus to the apocalyptic movement. Albert Schweitzer saw
Jesus as an apocalyptist: 'The eschatology of Jesus can there-
fore only be interpreted by the aid of the curiously inter-
mittent Jewish apocalyptic literature of the period between
Daniel and the Bar-Cochba rising.'[1] Not many have been able
to follow Schweitzer in his general approach, but there have
been some who have thought him right in linking Jesus with
apocalyptic. Quite recently Carl E. Braaten has spoken of the
'discovery of the apocalyptic Jesus'. In the light of this he
holds that the way forward for systematic theology is 'cheer-
fully to acknowledge the apocalypticism of Jesus and to make
it the point of departure and of central significance for systematic theology today'.[2]

Interestingly Käsemann, who has done so much to
emphasize the importance of apocalyptic for New Testament

[7] R. H. Charles, *The Apocrypha and Pseudepigrapha of the Old
Testament*, ii, p. vii. W. Förster also sees the destruction of the temple
as the dividing point. After that, Pharisaism 'concentrated explicitly
upon the "Law" and pushed wholly into the background the lines of
thought that we were able to trace out in Essenism and the apocalyptic
writings' (*Palestinian Judaism in New Testament Times*, Edinburgh
and London, 1964, p. 179).
[8] W. D. Davies, *Christian Origins and Judaism*, London, 1962, p. 25.
[9] *Ibid.*, p. 29. He goes on to suggest that different Rabbis may have
differed in their attitude to apocalyptic in much the same way as different
modern Christians differ in their attitude to the Second Advent. See
also his *Paul and Rabbinic Judaism*, London, 1948, pp. 9f.
[1] A. Schweitzer, *The Quest of the Historical Jesus*, London, 1945, p. 365.
[2] C. E. Braaten, in *Interpretation*, xxv, 1971, p. 482.

studies, does not go along with this. He sees primitive Christianity as resorting to 'apocalyptic terms as a means of responding to, and in a certain sense supplanting, Jesus' preaching of the nearness of God'.[3] He thus puts a marked break between what Jesus taught and what the early church taught, and it is the early church that he sees as markedly apocalyptic in its outlook.

Most students have found themselves unable to see Jesus as either an apocalyptist or as completely opposed to apocalyptic. They opt for a middling position. There are aspects of His ethical teaching, for example, which do not fit easily into apocalyptic (Schweitzer had to get rid of this by labelling it *Interimsethik*). But Jesus did make use of some apocalyptic expressions and apparently found some of its ideas congenial. His eschatology has undoubted points of contact with apocalyptic.

Our knowledge of apocalyptic has in recent days been enlarged by the discovery of the Qumran scrolls. The realization of the importance of apocalyptic for the Qumran community has stimulated interest in the whole subject and has helped us see how it might be of importance also as part of the background of the New Testament. The scrolls have revealed to us from the inside something of the thinking of a sect hitherto unknown. Many, of course, identify the men of Qumran with the Essenes. But even if the identification be accepted, the sect is still new, for we have no other information about Essene teaching from within the sect. The scrolls show among other things that the men of Qumran had a deep interest in apocalyptic. Among the writings the sect copied out and evidently held in high esteem are several apocalypses, for example, the *Book of Jubilees*, the *Testaments of the Twelve Patriarchs* and the *Book of Enoch*. The sect itself also produced works of a similar character, such as the *War Scroll*.

[3] E. Käsemann, in *Journal for Theology and the Church*, no. 6, 1969, p. 40. He thinks that if the validity of his statement about apocalyptic being the mother of Christian theology (quoted in my opening sentence) 'were to be repudiated and Jesus were to be regarded as more firmly bound up with the beginnings of Christian theology than seems to me to be justified, yet it would still be necessary to see in post-Easter apocalyptic a theological new beginning'.

It is plain that the information now brought to light about the thinking and practice of the men of Qumran underlines the importance of apocalyptic for their own sect and by implication for others. Apocalypticism did not originate with Qumran. While some of the members of the sect evidently did produce apocalyptic writings, they did not begin the genre. They simply carried on something that derived from outside. But if it was important to them, it was presumably important to others as well. The men of Qumran add their quota to the pile of evidence that shows that this type of thinking was widely popular.[4]

It should perhaps be emphasized that much of the present attitude of scholars to apocalyptic is recent. F. M. Cross cites a description of apocalyptic he himself made ten years ago and goes on to remark, it 'sounds archaic in my ears today'.[5] Albert Schweitzer awakened the theological world to the importance of eschatology years ago. His presentation was so one-sided that few were prepared to follow him whole-heartedly. But one result of his work was that eschatology assumed a new importance. After Schweitzer, few would be ready to deny the very great importance of eschatology, both in the teaching of Jesus and in that of His followers. Jesus could no longer be seen as a precursor of the modern liberal thinkers. He was a man of the first century, not the twentieth century. And He was interested in first-century eschatological ideas.

But eschatology and apocalyptic are not synonymous terms. Schweitzer had demonstrated that a deep eschatological concern ran through the New Testament. But to many scholars this was very different from the assertion that apocalyptic was a major influence on the New Testament preachers and writers. In the last few years the discovery of new texts and the realization of the relevance of some previously known texts are altering the whole situation.

That this subject is a live one today may be seen from the fact that a recent number of the periodical *Interpretation* was

---

[4] See further, W. Förster, *op. cit.*, pp. 74–81.

[5] F. M. Cross, in *Journal for Theology and the Church*, no. 6, 1969, p. 157.

given over entirely to this subject, as a year or two ago was a number of the *Journal for Theology and the Church* (from which our citations of Käsemann are taken). The editorial in *Interpretation* noted the 'rather vigorous discussion and debate during the past decade over the origins and nature of apocalyptic as well as its continuing theological meaning and usefulness'. It went on to point to the relevance of apocalyptic for the men of today. It saw as a common concern running through all the articles it published on this theme 'a very serious interest in the relationship of ancient apocalyptic to the theological and cultural situation of our time'.[6] It is thus more than ever important that the student of the New Testament (to say nothing of the student of the modern scene) have some understanding of what apocalyptic is. After this somewhat lengthy introduction, we accordingly turn to the nature of apocalyptic.

[6] *Interpretation*, xxv, 1971, p. 500.

THE MEANING OF APOCALYPTIC

The term 'apocalyptic' is derived from the Greek word *apokalypsis* (found in Rev. 1:1), which means 'uncovering' or 'revelation'. Literature bearing this name may thus be expected to be largely taken up with revealing what has been hidden. The term may be used in more ways than one. In the first instance it applies to a group of writings with certain characteristics which we shall note, mostly from the last two centuries BC and the first century AD. In the second place it denotes the ideas and concepts that are so characteristic of this kind of literature.[1] There may thus be 'apocalyptic' sections in writings which as a whole do not come within this category.

We should make it clear that 'apocalyptic' is our term. It is not one which the ancients used, at least in this way. It is not even certain that they regarded the books we speak of as apocalyptic as constituting a definite class. Doubtless they saw some similarities, but whether they were as impressed by them as are modern scholars, we do not know. If they were, they have not left it on record. There is quite a range of apocalyptic opinion, and the men who wrote this kind of literature seem to have come from all parties and from none. It may well not have occurred to the men of antiquity, according-ly, to group their writings together. They may have been more impressed by the differences than the resemblances. In

[1] The point is made by G. Ebeling, who sees it as 'necessary to distinguish between apocalyptic in the sense of the literary form known as "apocalypse", and apocalyptic in the sense of specific theological motifs' (*Journal for Theology and the Church*, no. 6, 1969, p. 52). In the same periodical Hans Dieter Betz remarks: 'In general we understand "apocalyptic" to apply to two things: first, a certain body of writings, the apocalypses, that is, revelatory writings which intend to reveal the secrets of the transcendental world and the end-time; second, it applies to the world of concepts and ideas which comes to expression in those texts' (*op. cit.*, p. 135).

antiquity then there is neither the name (*i.e.* as applied to a class of books;[2] the term occurs but is used otherwise), nor the classification. When we look for the characteristics of this class of books the ancients are no help to us.

One would have thought that a modern classification would be comparatively easy to handle. Since modern men have coined and used the term it would be natural to expect that they have a clear idea in mind as to what it should denote. This, however, proves not to be the case. While most are agreed that the term is valuable, because there is such a thing as apocalyptic, there is no consensus as to exactly what the term denotes. There is no agreed list of apocalyptic books and it is not easy to define what we mean by apocalyptic literature.

Now and then an attempt is made to describe it in terms of biblical literature. Thus J. L. Koole thinks it possible 'to present a description of the concept "apocalyptic literature". It is those Bible passages in which, at divine bidding, an organ of revelation (prophet or apostle) presents an account of the mystery of the future, especially of the latter days, as it is made known to him in a condition of ecstatic vision by means of symbolic figures and events.'[3] It is, however, much more usual to recognize that the name is applicable to a wide range of non-biblical literature and to seek its essential characteristics there.

C. C. Torrey lists as Jewish apocalypses the canonical book of Daniel, to which he adds *Enoch* (a composite work, with the oldest part written *c.* 120 BC); *Slavonic Enoch,* also called

---

[2] P. Vielhauer notices that the term occurs in the title of the Syrian *Baruch*: 'Book of the Revelation of Baruch, son of Neria, translated from Greek into Syriac'. But he points out that the Greek is itself a translation from an original Hebrew or Aramaic of the period AD 70–132: '. . . consequently we may regard the influence of Christian usage on the title of the Syriac translation as possible or even probable. The same is true of the title of the Greek Baruch. At all events, the use of the term "Revelation" to describe this literary work it not proved to be pre-Christian.' He adds, 'This literary genre does not appear originally to have had any common title' (E. Hennecke, *New Testament Apocrypha*, ed. W. Schneemelcher, trans. R. McL. Wilson, ii, London, 1965, p. 582).

[3] J. L. Koole, in *The Encyclopedia of Christianity*, i, ed. Edwin H. Palmer *et al.*, Wilmington, Delaware, 1964, p. 297.

the *Book of the Secrets of Enoch* (written probably in the first half of the first century AD; Torrey sees Gnostic elements in the book and points out as noteworthy features the seven heavens, the millennium and life after death); the *Assumption of Moses* (written about the beginning of the Christian era); *2 Esdras,* also called *4 Ezra* (the best specimen of a theological apocalypse); the *Apocalypse of Baruch* (dating from the beginning of the second century AD; though written originally in Hebrew or Aramaic it is preserved only in Syriac); the Greek *Apocalypse of Baruch* (from the latter part of the second century AD, and described by Torrey as a 'good example of a degenerate Apocalypse of the Enoch type'); the *Sibylline Oracles,* Books III–V (from *c.* 140 BC down to *c.* AD 80); the *Testaments of the Twelve Patriarchs* (probably first century AD, though others date them earlier; the apocalyptic parts are in the Testaments attributed to Levi and Naphtali); the *Life of Adam and Eve,* or in another recension, the *Apocalypse of Moses* (of uncertain date; contains little apocalyptic). He also lists as deserving mention, but with very little discussion, the *Book of Jubilees,* the *Ascension of Isaiah,* the *Apocalypse of Abraham,* the *Apocalypses of Elias and Zephaniah,* those of *Moses* and *Esdras,* of *Sedrachis,* of *Adam,* the *Testament of Abraham,* and the *Testaments of Abraham, Isaac, and Jacob.* Of Christian apocalypses he lists the *Revelation* and the *Shepherd of Hermas.*[4]

D. S. Russell lists seventeen apocalyptic books:[5]

The Book of Daniel
I Enoch 1–36, 37–71, 72–82, 83–90, 91–108
The Book of Jubilees
The Sibylline Oracles, Book III
The Testaments of the XII Patriarchs
The Psalms of Solomon
The Assumption of Moses
The Martyrdom of Isaiah
The Life of Adam and Eve, or *The Apocalypse of Moses*
The Apocalypse of Abraham

[4] C. C. Torrey, in *The Jewish Encyclopedia,* i, pp. 673f.
[5] D. S. Russell, *The Method and Message of Jewish Apocalyptic,* London, 1964, pp. 37f.

The Testament of Abraham
II Enoch, or *The Book of the Secrets of Enoch*
The Sibylline Oracles, Book IV
II Esdras (= *4 Ezra*)
II Baruch, or *The Apocalypse of Baruch*
III Baruch
The Sibylline Oracles, Book V.

He also points out that some of the writings among the Qumran scrolls have apocalyptic features, so deserve to be noticed. These are the following:

Commentaries on Isaiah, Hosea, Micah, Nahum, Habakkuk, Zephaniah and Psalm 37
The Zadokite Document (or the *Damascus Document*)
The Manual of Discipline (or the *Rule of the Community*)
The Rule of the Congregation
A Scroll of Benedictions
The Testimonies Scroll (or a *Messianic Anthology*)
Hymns (or *Psalms*) *of Thanksgiving*
The War of the Sons of Light Against the Sons of Darkness (or the *Rule for the Final War*)
The Book of Mysteries
A Midrash on the Last Days
A Description of the New Jerusalem
An Angelic Liturgy
The Prayer of Nabonidus and a Pseudo-Daniel Apocalypse
A Genesis Apocryphon.[6]

It is clear that the Qumran scrolls have added to our knowledge of this kind of literature. While it would perhaps be too much to describe the covenanters as an apocalyptic sect (they were interested in other things), there can be no doubt of their deep interest in this type of writing. The *War Scroll* is, for example, an apocalyptic work and the same description could be applied to certain other scrolls. The *Thanksgiving Psalms,* while not apocalyptic, yet do include a description of the 'pangs' that will come on Israel in the last days in language which is markedly apocalyptic in tone.

[6] *Ibid.,* p. 39.

Other writers give other lists. There is no point in trying to be exhaustive. But enough has been said to show that there is wide divergence as to what we should understand by the term 'apocalyptic'. To some extent this arises because on any showing apocalyptic grades off into other styles of writing. Many ancient books are partly apocalyptic and partly something else. Some students will accordingly stress the apocalyptic features and regard a given book as on the whole apocalyptic. Others will stress the differences and classify it differently. Since, then, there is no agreement as to exactly which books are apocalyptic and which not, it is not surprising that it is somewhat difficult to give the term an exact definition. The boundaries of apocalyptic are not well defined and those who know most about it are least apt to be dogmatic. But there are certain broad characteristics of the literature which goes by this name. At the very least, it is worth drawing attention to the kind of books that are in mind when the term is used, the general ideas which these books express, and the problems they raise.

THE MILIEU OF APOCALYPTIC

G. E. Ladd sees this class of literature as called forth by three main factors.[1] There is first the emergence of the 'Righteous Remnant'. This is an expression derived from the prophets, which a number of groups applied to themselves. Ladd cites the Chasidim, the Pharisees, and the men of Qumran as examples of groups who at one time or another saw themselves in this role. Whenever men found themselves in a minority group, faithfully serving God but with little prospect of the nation as a whole coming to see things from their point of view, there was a tendency for them to hold that the 'Righteous Remnant' prophecies were fulfilled in them. Even if prophecy was not held to be involved there was a mentality of a special kind in such minority groups and it found apocalyptic congenial. The literature it produced was essentially protest literature.

Paul D. Hanson expresses essentially the same point in a slightly different way when he denies that the apocalyptists formed a single party. He sees them as coming from a variety of circles, but as having as their common characteristic that they lacked power: 'whatever their party affiliation, the visionaries stem from the disenfranchised, especially those having fallen from positions of power'.[2] This scarcely does justice to the intense religious feeling of the apocalyptists (though Hanson recognizes this elsewhere). But it does emphasize an important feature of the apocalyptic outlook.

Ladd's second point is the problem of evil. In earlier days the simple viewpoint that God punished the wicked and rewarded the righteous seems to have sufficed. This accounted

[1] G. E. Ladd, art. 'Apocalyptic', in *Baker's Dictionary of Theology*, Grand Rapids, 1960.
[2] P. D. Hanson, in *Interpretation*, xxv, 1971, p. 474.

for enough of the facts to satisfy most Israelites for a long time. But after the Exile, Israel was restored to her own land, where she was more or less faithful in keeping the Law. She was not perfect, but most of the grosser offences of earlier days disappeared. For example, in the post-exilic period the nation was not notorious for idol worship. There was a marked tendency to stress the place of the Law and to try to obey God's commandments. At the very least it could be said that Israel lived on a higher moral plane than did most of her neighbours. But she was not prosperous. Instead, except for brief periods, she simply passed from subjection to one nation to subjection to another.

The third factor was the cessation of prophecy. Sometimes this is explicitly stated, *e.g.*, 'the prophets have fallen asleep' (*2 Baruch* 85:3). For centuries Israel had heard those spiritual giants thunder forth their denunciations of evil as they pointed the way to the service of God. But when the voice of prophecy fell silent there was the need for something to fill the vacuum. The apocalyptists spoke for God as best they knew. And if they did not reach the spiritual stature' of the prophets, that is not to be wondered at. Who did? We may still be grateful to the apocalyptists for their fervent advocacy of the cause of righteousness. So they wrote their books in the endeavour to bring a word of God to the need of the men of their day.

D. S. Russell sees the apocalyptic books as a record of difficult years

> not in terms of historical event, but in terms of the response of faith which the nation was called upon to make. They cannot be understood apart from the religious, political and economic circumstances of the times, nor can the times themselves be understood apart from these books whose hopes and fears echo and re-echo the faith of God's chosen people.[3]

The point is important. Apocalyptic was indeed called forth by the circumstances of the day. But it should not be understood in opportunistic terms, or in terms of worldly wisdom or

[3] D. S. Russell, *The Method and Message of Jewish Apocalyptic*. p. 16.

of fanatical piety. It was 'the response of faith', responding to the times, but also reacting in its turn on the times, for it built up faith in God's people. It was scarcely possible apart from the unusual times and circumstances in which it arose.

This combination of circumstances brought about a situation in which the new type of writing could flourish. It was directed mainly to a people in trouble, a people who saw themselves as God's own, but who were puzzled by the plight in which they found themselves. The apocalyptists sought to justify God's ways to men and to give courage and confidence to God's people. They put meaning into life for confused and troubled men. As William A. Beardslee puts it,

> Apocalyptic was a Judeo-Christian world-view which located the believer in a minority community and gave his life meaning by relating it to the end, soon to come, which would reverse his present status. The key to the interpretation of apocalyptic has usually been seen, rightly, in its restlessness with the imperfections of the present and its quest for a new and total solution to the human problem.[4]

Apocalyptic never flourished when life was easy and straightforward. But it made life livable for men under intolerable conditions with its emphasis on God's final and perfect solution.

There can be no doubt but that apocalyptic flourished in Jewish and Christian circles. But it is another question whether it originated there. H. H. Rowley thinks it did, and he says forthrightly: 'That apocalyptic is the child of prophecy, yet diverse from prophecy, can hardly be disputed.'[5] D. S. Russell likewise sees in the Old Testament prophets much that prepares the way for the apocalyptists. He discusses a number of passages and concludes that these prophecies

> cannot be called 'apocalyptic' in the sense that the name can be applied to books like Daniel and its successors, but

---

[4] W. A. Beardslee, in *Interpretation*, xxv, 1971, p. 424.
[5] H. H. Rowley, *The Relevance of Apocalyptic*, London, 1963, p. 15. C. K. Barrett also sees the roots of both Jewish and Christian apocalyptic as 'in Old Testament prophecy', though he admits that 'not a few

it can be said that they contain the 'stuff' from which
apocalyptic is made – the notion of divine transcendence,
the development of angelology, fantastic symbolism, cosmic imagery, the use of foreign mythology, reinterpretation
of prophecy, the visionary form of inspiration, a distinctly
literary form, cataclysm and judgment, the Day of the
Lord, the destruction of the Gentiles, the Coming of the
Golden Age, the messianic deliverer and the resurrection
of the dead. When at last the historical conditions for
growth were right, these seeds rapidly grew into full flower
in the colourful and diverse literature of Jewish apocalyptic.[6]

This is a lengthy list and seems to show that it is impossible
to regard apocalyptic as essentially foreign. It is fundamentally Jewish.

S. B. Frost, of course, worked out in detail the thesis that
apocalyptic was a development of prophecy. He sums up his
view in these words: '. . . in general, prophecy shifted its
eschatological interest from the outworking of history to the
end of time itself, and re-emerged as apocalyptic.'[7] There had
always been a prophetic interest in eschatology, but Frost saw
it as initially concerned with the historical process, as indeed
do most people. The Hebrews had a great interest in this
world and its history, and prophecy is fully in accordance
with this emphasis. But, Frost holds, at a later time circumstances caused many people to fix their gaze on the End, and
that was the beginning of apocalyptic. Actually Frost is not
fully consistent on this point, for he sometimes sees myth as
basic[8] and sometimes he sees un-Hebraic elements as when
he refers to 'the task of Hebrew-Babylonian synthetizing' and
goes on to say, 'although the apocalyptic school flourished
so strongly at the beginning of the Christian era, it was nevertheless always conscious of its exotic and alien origin'.[9] But

---

non-Jewish influences helped to shape its development' (*The New
Testament Background: Selected Documents*, London, 1957, p. 227).

[6] D. S. Russell, *op. cit.*, p. 91.

[7] S. B. Frost, *Old Testament Apocalyptic*, London, 1952, p. 83.

[8] See below, p. 32, n. 2.

[9] S. B. Frost, *op. cit.*, p. 86.

though he allows in this way for important infusions of ideas and methods from outside Hebrew prophecy, the main thrust of his book leaves us in no doubt but that Hebrew prophecy and not some other source is the true origin from which apocalyptic sprang.

Paul D. Hanson is another to work out the thesis that apocalyptic developed from prophecy. He sees the Hebrew prophets as preserving a tension between a 'realistic' and a 'visionary' activity. The prophet 'was called by Yahweh to straddle two worlds, to view the deliberation and events of the cosmic realm, but then immediately to integrate that vision into the events of the politico-historical order'.[1] The true prophet was thus a man of vision, but one who took this mundane temporal history with full seriousness. He expected that he would have to do things (as would other men), but the action of God would be seen in and through these actions. When this tension was not maintained, prophecy was replaced by something else. 'Prophetic eschatology is transformed into apocalyptic at the point where the task of translating the cosmic vision into the categories of mundane reality is abdicated.'[2] While not all will feel able to go along with Hanson's argument (I cannot accept it all myself), at least he has from another point of view drawn attention to the kinship between prophecy and apocalyptic. He thinks that 'the "tap-root" of apocalyptic lies in prophecy',[3] so must be grouped with Rowley and Russell as seeing apocalyptic as essentially a home-grown Jewish product.

R. G. Hamerton-Kelly has advanced a thesis that connects apocalyptic with yet another strand in Hebrew life, namely, the temple and its worship. He finds in apocalyptic 'a clear tradition of hostility to the temple of Jerusalem, coupled with

[1] P. D. Hanson, art. cit., p. 459.
[2] Ibid., p. 469. Eric Voegelin is another who sees prophecy as the basis of apocalyptic. He uses the term 'metastasis' to denote 'the change in the constitution of being envisaged by the prophets' (Order and History, vol. i, Israel and Revelation, Louisiana, 1969, p. 452), and he says, 'This metastatic component became so predominant in the complex phenomenon of prophetism that in late Judaism it created its specific symbolic form in the apocalyptic literature' (ibid., p. 453).
[3] P. D. Hanson, art. cit., p. 456.

a great concern for the temple as a religious idea'.[4] This is, of course, well illustrated in the case of the Qumran sectarians, but Hamerton-Kelly sees it elsewhere in apocalyptic circles as well. He does not argue that it is in those directly associated with the temple, the priests, and other officials, that apocalyptic has its essential being, but that 'apocalyptic arose in circles estranged from the theocracy by the temple – as well as by eschatology'.[5] There is much that is suggestive in his article, and, without committing ourselves to the entire argument, we may yet agree that in much apocalyptic there is a love for the temple coupled with a profound conviction that those responsible for running it are doing so in a manner contrary to the divine ordinance. We need not doubt that many apocalyptists, including some early ones, were opposed to the temple authorities, though interested in priestly affairs. It may well be that if we are to understand apocalyptic aright we must take account of the priestly tradition as well as the prophetic and perhaps other traditions as well. Apocalyptic has a complex background. Though he differs greatly from writers like those we have so far considered, Hamerton-Kelly lends support to those who see apocalyptic as thoroughly Jewish in origin.

However, some scholars, particularly continental scholars, deny that it is. Thus Betz sees apocalyptic as part of a great movement throughout the Hellenistic world of the day. He adopts a religio-historical approach and looks for parallels to apocalyptic ideas and expressions in a number of Hellenistic sources. On the basis of this research he decides that 'Jewish and, subsequently, Christian apocalypticism as well cannot be understood from themselves or from the Old Testament alone, but must be seen and presented as peculiar expressions within the entire development of Hellenistic syncretism'.[6]

Betz cites an interesting array of parallels and makes it likely that the influence on apocalyptic of ideas and expressions from the richly endowed field of Hellenism has been underestimated. But it is more than doubtful whether he has

[4] R. G. Hamerton-Kelly, in *Vetus Testamentum*, xx, 1970, p. 1.
[5] *Ibid.*, p. 15.
[6] H. D. Betz, in *Journal for Theology and the Church*, no. 6, 1969, p. 155.

really shaken Rowley's position. The parallels he adduces are often so inexact that we need not postulate syncretistic Hellenism as the necessary background to the world of apocalyptic. It may well have given apocalyptic some of its forms of expression, but it has yet to be shown that it was in any real sense determinative.[7]

Others argue with a greater show of plausibility that apocalyptic is not so much a general Hellenistic phenomenon as a development from Iranian religion.[8] As we will see later, dualism is very characteristic of apocalyptic and a strong case has been made out for seeing dependence on Iranian dualism accordingly. Gerhard Gloege thinks that Daniel 'uses ideas that come from outside, from the religion of the Persian Zarathustra, and to some extent also from Babylonian religion'.[9] He gives as examples of what he has in mind the ideas of the four ages of the world, of the resurrection and judgment and of the heavenly 'Man'.

A difficulty in the way of all such views is that apocalyptic is a stubbornly Jewish and Christian development. This type of literature flourished (the word is not too strong) in a Jewish environment, but we see nothing comparable in any other environment known to us. It is also the case that the characteristic concepts of this literature are not really found elsewhere, at least as far as it is known at present. We may think of Iranian dualism as perhaps influencing the apocalyptic doctrine of the two ages. But the expectation of the near end of the present age and the imminence of that to come, which is such a feature of apocalyptic, does not appear to be Iranian. This kind of comment could be made often. Apocalyptic has been influenced by ideas from non-Jewish sources, but so far

[7] Beardslee agrees that there are syncretistic elements in apocalyptic. But he maintains that 'Betz's sampling of the data is too limited for him to have yet made a convincing case' (*Interpretation*, xxv, 1971, p. 435, n. 31).

[8] *Cf.* H. Conzelmann, 'The most important problem from the point of view of the history of religion is that of the origin of apocalyptic. Persian influence is determinative' (*An Outline of the Theology of the New Testament*, London, 1969, p. 23).

[9] G. Gloege, *The Day of His Coming*, London, 1963, p. 56. Gloege does not see Daniel as essentially Iranian or Babylonian, so he can say 'the seer does not work in a Persian or Babylonian spirit; his is the old prophetic spirit' (*ibid.*).

it has not been shown that its characteristic ideas are deriv-
able from any such non-Jewish source.

F. M. Cross roots apocalyptic quite firmly in a Hebrew
milieu, though he does not connect it with prophecy as do
Rowley and Barrett. He takes it back further and sees other
influences as also important, and in each case it should be
noted that they are Hebrew influences. It is in 'late exilic
and early post-exilic literature that we detect the rudimentary
traits and motives of apocalypticism'.[1] In a footnote to this
statement he says:

> With the recovery of the Canaanite mythic and epic poetry,
> certain judgments about the character of apocalyptic syn-
> cretism must be modified. It has become vividly clear that
> the primary source of mythic material informing Jewish
> apocalyptic was *old* Canaanite mythic lore. This, of course,
> is not to dispense with all resort to Iranian, Mesopotamian,
> or Greek borrowings in describing the evolution of apoca-
> lyptic. It does mean, however, that many apocalyptic tradi-
> tions go back through earliest Israel to Canaanite sources
> so that more continuities with the old biblical community
> must be recognized rather than fewer.[2]

Nobody seems to have disposed of the stubborn fact that
apocalyptic is a Jewish and Christian phenomenon. It is hard
to see this literature as derived from a source which does not
know it. Granted that there have been borrowings from many
sources, the main idea is surely Jewish. Even if Cross's idea
be accepted that much goes back ultimately to old Canaanite,
we still look for an explanation of why, if this is the essential

[1] F. M. Cross, in *Journal for Theology and the Church*, no. 6, 1969,
p. 165.
[2] *Ibid.*, p. 165, n. 23. S. B. Frost also emphasizes the place of myth, and
for example says, 'Apocalyptic is the result of the eschatologizing of
Semitic myth, or to put it more truly, the result of Hebrew eschatology
expressing itself in terms of semitic myth' (*op. cit.*, p. 76). He can speak
of apocalyptic as 'mythologized eschatology' (*ibid.*, p. 39; *cf.* pp. 247f.).
The revised Hastings one-volume *Dictionary of the Bible* likewise finds
an amalgam of various sources including myth: 'In the apocalypse we
thus can see a union of the symbolism and myths of Babylonia with the
religious faith of the Jews, under the influence of Hellenistic culture'
(*loc. cit.*).

story, we have to wait so long for the appearance of this class of literature. It does not appear in the Canaanite so far known to us and it does not appear in Israelite literature for centuries after the settlement in Canaan. There is clearly more to the story than old Canaan. It is better to see apocalyptic as gathering in from many sources, both old and new, but as being basically of Jewish origin.

It may or may not, as Rowley holds, be derived from prophecy. As we will see in a later section, von Rad stresses the connection with the Wisdom literature and thinks this the true origin of apocalyptic. Perhaps in our present state of knowledge it is wise not to be dogmatic. Fully developed apocalyptic is a Jewish and Christian affair. We may discern influences that have gone to shaping it and these come from a variety of sources. But there is none that we can postulate with absolute confidence as the origin of apocalyptic.

Revelations

Usually the apocalyptic writers tell of revelations made to their heroes. Indeed the very name 'apocalypse' means 'revelation', as we have already seen. The writer of an apocalypse tends to choose some great man of the past and make him the centre of the book (a good deal of literature clusters round the names of Enoch and Noah, and again of Moses and of Ezra, the second Moses). Not uncommonly this great one speaks the words of the book. Sometimes he has visions which he narrates (and which convey the message for the writer's own day). Not uncommonly he goes on a journey with an angel or other celestial guide who shows him interesting sights and comments on them. At the very least there are interviews with heavenly personages. Some maintain that vision is characteristic of apocalypse and audition of prophecy. This may perhaps stand as a rough generalization. But it should not be overlooked that it breaks down in both directions. Some of the prophets had visions and some of the apocalyptists had auditions. But it is certainly the case that among the apocalyptists visions predominate.

The revelations cover a wide range of subjects. Commonly there is a concentration on the end-time, and we read a good deal about the way this world will be brought to a close and the kingdom of God ushered in. But the revelation might be concerned with the secrets of heaven, or with the explanation of natural phenomena. Or its subject might be history, which may take in anything from creation to the coming of Messiah and may indeed cover this whole range in short compass. Sometimes we are given information about the characters and deeds of angels, both good and bad. Or we may be told

about final judgment and given information about events
leading up to it. Heaven and hell, which follow it, are sometimes described, as is the Messianic kingdom. The variety of
topics is very wide. The one thing in common appears to be
that these are things that could not be known naturally. They
had to be the subject of special revelation. And in apocalyptic
this normally means special revelation to some hero of the
faith of past days.

A feature of the revelation is its esoteric character. Often
it is explicitly said that it is to be kept secret until the last
days, which, of course, turn out to be the apocalyptist's own
times. And when it is made known, apocalyptic is scarcely
literature for the masses. It cannot ever have been easy to
interpret in detail, and it properly belongs within a sect or
party. It is for 'the wise', those initiated (not necessarily in
any formal sense) into the apocalyptic group.

It is often said that this is a somewhat indirect way of
arriving at God's word for the situation, and that in this
apocalyptic contrasts with prophecy. The characteristic of the
prophets was that they could say, 'Thus saith the Lord.' They
had an immediate experience of God, and they told of that
experience in direct, forthright words. The apocalyptists, by
contrast, made no claim to this direct experience.[1] While
they were sure that what they wrote was a message from God
to the men of their own day and generation, yet they occupied
a secondary position compared with that of the prophets.
They looked to an angel or other intermediary as the source
of their information. Angels are especially prominent.

But this may be too simple. In fact, in some apocalypses the
writer tells us that God did speak directly to him (e.g. the
Book of the Secrets of Enoch, 2 Baruch, etc.). While the typical apocalyptist may well interpose an intermediary between
himself and the message of God, this rule is broken often
enough to be significant. Perhaps, however, even when it is
so broken there is a difference from the prophets. The typical
prophet has an urgent ethical imperative the apocalyptist

---

[1] Cf. A. Oepke: 'Judaism forged a certain substitute for living revelation
in apocalyptic' (Theological Dictionary of the New Testament, ed.
G. Kittel, trans. G. W. Bromiley, iii, Grand Rapids, 1965, p. 578).

does not have. He has a sense that God, none less, has spoken, and men must accept God's word with awe. This does not seem to be characteristic of apocalyptic. Even when God is the speaker in the apocalypses, an angel could usually have said much the same without appreciable difference. Indeed, when God speaks there is a tendency for the apocalyptists to see Him as giving much the same kind of explanation or teaching as do angels in other apocalypses. The awe-inspiring authoritative divine pronouncement is rarely found. The sense of having 'stood in the council of the Lord' (Je. 23:18) is distinctive of the prophets and is scarcely to be found if at all in the apocalyptists.

This is not to say that these latter think they are giving no more than the word of man in their situation. They normally regard the content of their writings as beyond the ability of human ingenuity to search out. In one way or another their books deal with the purpose of God. Sometimes this is seen in the past, it is true, where it may be discerned by any. But sometimes also it is in historical events yet to take place, and sometimes it is in heaven or some other extra-terrestrial sphere. Sometimes we are given information about the activities of good or evil spirits, or about the phenomena of nature. All this shows that the apocalyptists did not think of themselves as uttering commonplaces. They saw their message as revealed and their role as that of giving a word from God to the men of their day. But they did not have the same awareness of the immediate presence of God as did the great prophets. There is qualitative difference.

Symbolism

A feature of much apocalyptic that often makes it unintelligible to modern men is the use of strange symbolism. So typical is this that E. Schürer could regard it as the characteristic feature:

The peculiarity of this later 'apocalyptic' medium as distinguished from the older genuine prophecy is this, that it imparts its revelations not in clear and plain language, but in a mysterious *enigmatical form*. The thing intended to be communicated is veiled under parables and symbols, the meaning of which can only be guessed at.[2]

This type of literature abounds in beasts and seals, in rivers and mountains and stars, in personages celestial and infernal. The symbols may change in bewildering fashion. Thus in *I Enoch* we read of stars falling from heaven and becoming bulls. They cohabit with cows and sire elephants, camels, and asses (*I Enoch* 86:1–4). Later we learn of a white bull that became a man (*I Enoch* 89:1), and of bulls which sired creatures as diverse as lions, tigers, wolves, squirrels, vultures and others (*I Enoch* 89:10). Such wonders are found over and over. It may be that some of it was derived from the dream life of the apocalyptists, but much is found in a number of different authors and must be regarded as more or less conventional. Thus beasts often stand for people, horns for kings, and stars or men for angels.

Paradoxically this use of conventional symbols does not mean that the apocalyptists were not transmitting genuine experiences of their own. As Th. Mann puts it,

There is in fact an apocalyptic culture which transmits to the ecstatics visions and experiences which are to a certain degree fixed, – however much it may appear as a psychological curiosity that someone gives frenzied expression to what someone else has previously communicated to him in a frenzied state, and that people are raptured, not independently, but in something like a process of borrowing, and according to a mechanical routine. Nevertheless this is the position.[3]

They had genuine experiences but these come to us in an accepted terminology which may show that the same experience befell numbers of individuals of a similar outlook.

Russell argues strongly that the apocalyptists record

[2] E. Schürer, *A History of the Jewish People in the Time of Jesus Christ*, II, iii, Edinburgh, 1886, pp. 46f.
[3] Cited by P. Vielhauer in *New Testament Apocrypha*, ii, p. 584 (from *Doctor Faustus*, p. 567).

genuinely personal experiences. He cites a number of passages from a variety of apocalypses which describe in vivid language mental and physical phenomena said to have been experienced by the great one in whose name the revelation is recorded. Russell proceeds, 'All these experiences are so true psychologically that it is difficult to see in them nothing more than the expression of literary convention; their very nature argues strongly that they reflect the actual experiences of the apocalyptic writers themselves.'[4] The point should be taken with full seriousness at the same time as we realize that much of the imagery is repeated in a number of apocalypses. Sometimes, we may be sure, the apocalyptists simply used conventional imagery with no thought of recording a genuine experience. But the point made by both Mann and Russell is that on other occasions they record genuine personal experiences, even though they use the same imagery as do others.[5]

Sometimes the meaning of the symbolism is fairly plain. But unfortunately more often the modern reader can make neither head nor tail of it. The apocalyptists did not always (or even usually) think it necessary to explain their symbolism. There appear to have been times when it would have been politically unwise for them to have done so. They evidently trusted that their friends would be able to discern their essential meaning, and that their enemies would not be able to do so. Part of their reason for using bizarre symbolism will also be that they were trying to describe something that was too big for words. After all, their main theme was the end of the world, and this is something for which we have no adequate language. In the nature of the case there are no parallels. So the apocalyptists used symbolism as their subject practically compelled them to do.

[4] D. S. Russell, *The Method and Message of Jewish Apocalyptic*, pp. 165f.
[5] *Cf.* Amos N. Wilder, 'I am convinced that this cultural medium of writing nevertheless incorporates mimetic and ecstatic utterance and formulas, whether originating in his own vision or in ancient hierophanies quickened in his own imaginative act' (*Interpretation*, xxv, 1971, p. 446). He also cites Lars Hartman, '. . . an author who uses well-established, conventional literary forms for rendering visions may nevertheless cast his own visionary experiences in precisely these forms which he has taken over' (*ibid.*, n. 21).

It is quite possible that within certain Jewish circles a generally accepted symbolism was widely understood. This would be supported by the way different apocalypses make use of the same kind of imagery. C. C. Torrey finds 'one of the most noticeable features in the history of this literature' in 'the constancy with which its own traditions are maintained'. He goes on, 'Phraseology, imagery, and modes of thought or interpretation are passed on from hand to hand.'[6] It seems as if some at any rate of the fantastic world of beasts and heavenly portents and angels was shared by a wide circle who apparently could readily comprehend what was meant. Yet we must bear in mind that the same symbol could mean different things in different apocalypses. While there was continuity there was also development.

Perhaps we should notice that numbers were often employed symbolically. We frequently meet the numerals 3, 4, 7, 10, 12, and multiples of any of them. Seventy is very common in a variety of Jewish books while in the Christian book of Revelation the number seven keeps recurring. The apocalyptists loved schematism, and the constant use of numerical patterns is a feature of their systems.

Symbolism and significant numbers, then, abound. Whether they explain them or not, the apocalyptists use their bizarre symbolism and their curious numerology consistently. Any student of these writings must make an effort to grapple with the phenomenon.

Pessimism

There is a pessimistic strain in this literature generally, and sometimes the apocalyptists are said without qualification to be pessimists. This estimate must be taken with caution, but there is a sense in which it is true. The apocalyptists wrote to a people who were in difficulties. D. N. Freedman sees this type of literature as 'born of crisis – from the start it was underground literature, the consolation of the persecuted'.[7]

[6] C. C. Torrey, in *The Jewish Encyclopedia*, i, p. 672.
[7] D. N. Freedman, in *Journal for Theology and the Church*, no. 6, 1969, p. 173.

The apocalyptists certainly believed that 'man's extremity is God's opportunity' and they were confident that God would eventually intervene. But until that time came, things were hopeless. They saw no solution within the framework of human endeavour. They had no faith in progress. They did not believe there would be an orderly evolution to a better state of affairs.

Their attitude to rebellion is not uniform. Their distrust of man's ability to solve his problems should have led them to hold that rebellion, just as much as any other human activity, was hopeless, and clearly some did take this line. But others thought differently. During the period when apocalyptic flourished there were men who raised the standard of revolt against the entrenched authorities, and on occasion they were inspired at least in part by the apocalyptists. They evidently took to heart that strand of apocalyptic teaching which saw God as intervening in the last days and felt sure that they were living in the last times. The wild visions of apocalyptic spurred them on to heroic endeavour. If they struck the first blow, they seem to have reasoned, no doubt God would stand by them.

But God cannot be compelled to act in accordance with this kind of reasoning and there were disasters. Jerusalem was destroyed in AD 70 and again in the war of AD 132–135. Indeed, many believe that it was these disasters which finally discredited apocalyptic and that this was the basic reason for its cessation. Militant apocalypticism was tried in the fires of war and found wanting.

Be that as it may, some at any rate of the writers of apocalyptic must have discouraged armed intervention, for they put no trust in human endeavour. For them it was a basic truth that most men were on the wrong path and that accordingly they would never put their efforts behind the cause of right. Evil was powerful in the affairs of men. This world was in a bad state and it would get worse. This was an inevitable process. Sometimes this is emphasized with the thought of a time of especially great trouble right at the end of this age (cf. Dn. 12:1). The 'woes of the Messiah' were conceived of as a period of great distress just before the coming of the

Messiah. Wars, famines, earthquakes and other disasters are often mentioned. Right till the end of this present age the apocalyptists could discern nothing but trouble for a sinful world.

And when the new age is ushered in they did not envisage the majority of mankind as sharing in it. 'This age the Most High has made for many, but the age to come for few' (*4 Ezra* 8:1). Not only are most men sinners, but they will continue so to be and they will suffer accordingly in the final overthrow of evil. While the triumph of good is sure, it will be realized in only a minority of men.

The shaking of the foundations

The apocalyptists' pessimism did not arise from some passing discomfort. They were men whose whole world seemed to be crashing about their heads. Paul D. Hanson speaks of 'the crisis sociologists find at the base of every apocalyptic movement: the collapse of a well-ordered world view which defines values and orders the universe for a people, thrusting them into the unchartered chaos of anomie and meaninglessness'.[8] It was this that gripped the apocalyptists with whom we are dealing. The well-ordered world of the monarchy had long since passed away. Even the Exile had meant stability of a kind, and the days immediately after the return were, by comparison with what came later, well ordered.

But when little Judah found herself caught up in the conflict of world empires, the times were out of joint. She might enjoy her moments of triumph, as under the Maccabees, but these were all too rare. And they did not give the time or the opportunity for the development of the kind of ordered life in which a man may settle into a routine confident that God's in His heaven and all's right with the world. For the apocalyptist God might indeed be in His heaven, but all was far from being right in the world. And as far as he could see it never would be, short of catastrophic divine intervention.

He was caught up in changing values as well as in the clash

8 P. D. Hanson, in *Interpretation*, xxv, 1971, p. 455.

of arms and the clash of empires. There was a clash of cultures as Hellenism came in like a flood. The simplistic view that all would come out well for those who served God faithfully did not seem to be working. The result was that many were troubled exceedingly. The apocalyptists were thus not lamenting a sorry state of affairs that would, they hoped, soon be put right. Part of their trouble was the deep-seated conviction that there was no way on earth of its ever being put right unless and until God should intervene and destroy the whole world order.

So out of the greatness of their despair they envisaged the greatness of God's intervention. Amos N. Wilder puts a great deal of emphasis on the total character of the apocalyptic crisis. He points out that men can use extravagant language over small losses ('whether a baby rattle or a bank account, whether our sense of class or national pride, or our sense of how things should be generally'). 'But one should be able to tell the difference between the tantrums of a romantic who cannot bring the world to heel and the impersonal voice which speaks out of the crucible where the world is made and unmade.'[9]

A little later he describes true apocalyptic this way:

Common to all true apocalyptic is a situation characterized by anomie, a loss of 'world', or erosion of structures, psychic and cultural, with the consequent nakedness to Being or immediacy to the dynamics of existence. Hence the rhetorics of this 'panic' exposure in which all is at stake, involving antinomies of life and death, light and darkness, knowledge and nescience, order and chaos. And it can never be only a question of the individual. It is a juncture which renews the archaic crisis of all existence: that of survival, the viability of life.[1]

We should be clear that the true apocalyptist is seeing clear-sightedly a crisis of the uttermost magnitude. He is talking about the final breaking up of everything that is familiar,

[9] *Ibid.*, p. 440.
[1] *Ibid.*, pp. 440f. *Cf.* also, 'In this situation of disorientation, vertigo, and weightlessness there are not only no answers; there are no categories, no questions' (*ibid.*, p. 444).

the destruction of a whole way of life, even of a whole universe. It is true that he sees also that God is supreme even then, and out of chaos He will bring order. But we do not understand apocalyptic until we see its authors as wrestling with the ultimate disaster.[2]

The triumph of God

They look for catastrophe but it is a mistake to call the apocalyptists pessimists and stop there. Absolutely characteristic of this class of literature is the thought that in His own good time God will intervene. He will bring the present evil world to a cataclysmic end and establish a better state of affairs. The absolute rule of God is the significant thing. W. Sanday says,

> The fundamental idea of all apocalypse is really one that goes back far in the history of Israel, and is found in germ as soon as men began to reflect upon the nature of Monarchy, and in particular of Hebrew Monarchy. There soon grew up the conception to which Josephus gave the name of 'theocracy'. The rightful King of Israel was God; the human king was at best only God's vicegerent. The age when as yet there was no king in Israel was idealised, and hope for the future took the form of a restoration of that ideal condition.[3]

It is well for us to be reminded of the continuity of apocalyptic with earlier Israelite thought in this matter.

Yet we must also bear in mind that apocalyptic introduced an other-worldly dimension that is not stressed earlier. It may be found in the prophets, as in the new heaven and earth (Is. 66:22). But more characteristically the prophets are inter-

[2] Paul D. Hanson has a relevant comment about modern apocalyptists: 'This world-weariness has been the mark of every apocalyptic movement. It is shared today by men of vision who find a harshly brutal world denying them the opportunity to integrate their vision into the institutions of the historical realm. For them, too, myth often becomes a source of repose from a reality which they find too brutal to integrate into their apocalyptic vision' (*ibid.*, p. 479).

[3] W. Sanday, in *The Hibbert Journal*, x, 1911-12, p. 96.

ested in what takes place on this present earth. They are
interested in the resolution of present difficulties and they
concentrate on national hopes and the like. By contrast the
apocalyptists put their emphasis on the next world. In that
world, not this, God's purposes would be worked out fully.[4]

The apocalyptists differed widely in detail. They were not
sure when the End would be, though they usually thought it
would take place not far in the future from their own standpoint. Sometimes this was expressed in words of great power
and beauty, *e.g.* 'For the youth of the world is past; the
strength of the creation has long ago come to its end, and the
approach of the times is (already) at hand and (indeed already) passed by. For the pitcher is near to the well, the ship
to harbour, the caravan to the city, and life to its conclusion.'[5]
Such words graphically express the conviction that the end
of the world is very near indeed.

The apocalyptists differed as to how the End would be
brought about. They were not even agreed as to what the
ultimate outcome would be. Some looked for a kingdom on
this earth, and some thought this earth would be done away
and that a new heaven and a new earth would make their
appearance.[6] Some looked for a Messiah and some did not.
Again to quote Sanday,

> Sometimes God Himself was to reign upon earth; some-
> times He was to reign, not in person, but through His
> Viceroy, the Davidic King, His Anointed or Messiah. There
> was not felt to be the slightest antagonism between these

[4] L. H. Brockington speaks of 'a catastrophic intervention in the affairs
of men by God who dwells apart from it' and he sees the apocalyptic writers as 'writing of things that in effect belong to God's world,
that other world so far removed from this'; he goes on to speak of 'God's
aloofness' (*A Critical Introduction to the Apocrypha*, London, 1961,
pp. 151f.).

[5] *2 Baruch* 85:10 (cited from P. Vielhauer, in *New Testament Apocrypha*,
ii, p. 593). The idea that the world is old is found again in *4 Ezra* 5:55;
14:10, 16.

[6] The strand of apocalyptic that looks for a new heaven and a new earth
makes a great appeal to some modern apocalyptists. They are delighted
with a theology that makes cosmic interests integral to God's final purpose and contrasts these ancient thinkers with our generation which has
done so much to pollute its environment.

two ideals; they might quite well exist, and they did exist, side by side.[7]

Perhaps we should add that the Messianic kingdom, where it appeared, was normally a kingdom on this earth. It was a temporary affair, spanning the time between the end of this world's kingdoms and the setting up of God's final order. A point Christians are apt to get wrong, taking as they do Jesus Christ as the pattern of the Messiah, is that where the apocalypses do speak of a messiah he is usually a man like other men, often with nothing remarkable about him. Indeed Frost can differentiate the Son of man in the Parables of *1 Enoch* from the messiah elsewhere by saying, 'If he *is* the Messiah, then from being a complete nonentity he has at one bound become the *sine qua non* of the eschatological scene.'[8] The messiah then might be 'a complete nonentity' or this glorious Son of man. There was tremendous variety in the details of how the End would take place and what it would mean.

But absolutely fundamental is the thought that in the end God will prevail. He will overthrow all the evil this world contains. The apocalyptists were just as sure that God could and would defeat every evil man and every evil thing as they were that even the best efforts of good men could not bring this about. Their pessimism about men's efforts was balanced by a corresponding optimism about what God would do. They never lost their confident hope in the ultimate triumph of God. So characteristic is this that C. F. D. Moule can come close to defining apocalyptic in terms of it: 'Apocalypse – the anticipatory raising of the curtain to display the final scene – is a way of conveying, pictorially and in symbol, the conviction of the ultimate victory of God.'[9]

As they looked around them they saw the righteous oppressed and with no way out of their troubles. Humanly speaking there was no hope. But this did not weaken their faith in the slightest. The salvation they looked for would not be in the here and now but in an age yet to come. Thus the

[7] W. Sanday, *art. cit.*, p. 97.

[8] S. B. Frost, *Old Testament Apocalyptic*, p. 240.

[9] C. F. D. Moule, *The Birth of the New Testament*, London, 1962, p. 103.

troubles of the present age were quite irrelevant to the final triumph of good. It was unfortunate for those going through these troubles that there was no earthly hope for them. But they could be sustained by the eternal hope that burned brightly for the apocalyptists. Better to put up with troubles in this present life and make sure of a place with God in the blessedness to come than to join with the wicked and face eternal ruin.

This involved the thought of final judgment. Indeed so characteristic is the idea of judgment at the end time that F. C. Burkitt could say: 'It is this Divine Event that is set forth by the Apocalypses. The doctrine of the Apocalypses is the doctrine of the Last Judgment.'[1] Men cannot get away with their evil deeds, for judgment is certain. A corollary of this is the doctrine of personal immortality, and the apocalyptists put a good deal of stress on this. They looked for a blessed future life in which the people of God would enjoy the blessing of God with nothing to hinder their enjoyment. As long as men were shut up to this life as the sphere in which God operated there were difficulties posed by the triumph of the wicked. The apocalyptists purchased their liberation from these difficulties at the price of handing over this world to the evil one. They were ready to concede to the wicked all the success they could attain in the here and now. But they held firmly to the view that this is not the only nor the more important segment of living. In due course this present evil age will cease, and when the final state of events is ushered in it is the righteous who will triumph. And their triumph will not last for a few brief moments. It will be for eternity. Their whole system would have been impossible without the thought of immortality for the individual.

Sometimes the apocalyptists tried to put a date on all this. They usually felt that the End was not far away. They saw themselves as living in the last days and their task as that of preparing the people for an imminent end to all things. This no doubt had the effect of heightening interest in their message. But it involved a corresponding disillusionment when their prophecies did not come to pass. Rabbi Samuel B.

[1] F. C. Burkitt, *Jewish and Christian Apocalypses*, London, 1914, p. 2.

Nahmani passed on a bitterly critical saying of Rabbi Jonathan: 'Blasted be the bones of those who calculate the end. For they would say, since the predetermined time has arrived and yet he (*i.e.* the Messiah) has not come, he will never come.'[2] This sharp criticism is probably aimed at the apocalyptists. The Rabbis must have been very displeased when men began to abandon hope in the coming of the Messiah (a hope which meant a good deal to the Rabbis) on account of unfulfilled apocalyptic speculations.

Determinism

Allied to the idea of present evil to be followed by the final triumph of good is the rigid determinism so characteristic of this class of literature. For the apocalyptists it was clear that the course of this world's history is pre-ordained. They were not unduly perturbed by the power of evil about them, for they held that it was all part of the divine plan. As we have already seen, this had the unfortunate consequence that men could never hope to defeat the evil they encountered. But this did not engender an attitude of defeatism. The apocalyptists were not in the slightest dismayed, for they saw it as certain that this evil could not finally be triumphant. Its course was prescribed. It would have its little day. But then inevitably, inexorably it would perish.

This message was of immense value to the suffering righteous. Suffering has always been a problem to those who hold that God is both good and almighty. The people of God had usually in antiquity been taught that God would punish evil and reward good. It was, then, a special problem for the righteous when they saw evil men triumphant while they themselves were suffering deprivation and persecution. It was all so meaningless. There was nothing in the traditional approach that helped them. The tortured reasonings of Job and his comforters show us the kind of thing that must have gone on in the minds of many who could not solve the problem. In that particular book the climax is the vision

[2] *Sanhedrin* 97b (Soncino translation).

of God. No answer to the problem is given in set terms, but as Job draws near to God the problem falls away. The solution is in Him. But not all Israelites saw this. They agonized over the problem and found it perplexing in the extreme.

One great merit of the apocalyptic approach was that it did give meaning to the world's agony. The apocalyptists maintained that the hand of God was in it all. He had determined the course of events, and all must happen just as He had planned. The righteous might not understand all the workings of this plan, but they could understand that the plan existed and that their sufferings somehow fitted into it. The course of events must go as it was determined. This meant that the righteous could not expect their righteousness to save them here and now. Indeed, precisely on account of their righteousness they might well have to suffer all the more during the temporary triumph of evil. But nothing could interfere with the working out of what had been determined. Ultimately the triumph would come. Nothing could be more certain than that.

A feature of the apocalyptic approach is the use of great historical epochs associated often with the use of numbers. Thus there may be weeks of years (as in Daniel), or world history may be divided into seven thousand years (*Testament of Abraham*). The *Book of Jubilees,* as its name shows, puts its emphasis on the idea of jubilee in the Old Testament and surveys history in terms of 'jubilees' (though the author has forty-nine years, *i.e.* 7×7, in his jubilee instead of fifty as in the Old Testament). There are other schemes, for the apocalyptists show versatility and ingenuity in this matter. The number and the duration of all such epochs were seen as determined by God. He had planned them all and history was but the unfolding of His plan.[3] Men, it is true, are often

[3] This was a new thought. W. Eichrodt holds that 'at the decisive point the apocalyptists completely transform the ancient periodic system. When after the passing of the iron age the golden ought to return, and the cycle begin afresh, something entirely new is introduced, the eternal kingdom which comes down from heaven, bringing with it the final conclusion of earthly history' (*Theology of the Old Testament,* ii, London, 1967, p. 173).

thought of as having personal freedom (*e.g.* 2 *Baruch* 85:7), and they are to be blamed for their misdeeds as well as worthy of praise when they do well. But their freedom is exercised within the divinely ordained framework. Nothing can interfere with the working out of God's purpose.

Dualism

Apocalyptic in general makes considerable use of dualism. The thought is taken very seriously that 'the Most High has made not one world but two' (2 *Esdras* 7:50). Thus the present suffering is contrasted with the future salvation. Evil and good are constantly set over against one another, as are evil spirits and good spirits. The imagery of light and darkness is employed, black is set over against white. God is seen as in opposition to Satan, God's people as opposed to the heathen. This age is contrasted with the age to come, this world with the kingdom of God. R. H. Fuller sees in this latter point the characteristic of this type of literature: '. . . unlike prophecy, apocalyptic portrays that culmination not in this-worldly terms, but in a new heaven and a new earth. It envisages two ages, this age and the age to come. It is this transcendental element which marks the salient difference between prophecy and apocalyptic.'[4]

It should perhaps be pointed out that the world to come is sharply differentiated from this present age. It is not simply that it follows this age, it is qualitatively different. As Vielhauer puts it, '. . . *this Age* is temporary and perishable, the *Age to come* is imperishable and eternal'.[5] The age when God's will is perfectly done stands in sharp contrast with this imperfect age when there is so much evil confronting the servants of God. There were possibly occasions when the Israelites looked forward to a coming world that would be

---

[4] R. H. Fuller, *A Critical Introduction to the New Testament*, London, 1966, p. 184. Similarly G. von Rad says, 'The characteristic of apocalyptic theology is its eschatological dualism' (*Old Testament Theology*, ii, London, 1965, pp. 301f.).
[5] P. Vielhauer, in *New Testament Apocrypha*, ii, p. 588.

this world over again and with Israel triumphant, but this is not the vision of the apocalyptists. They thought of a new heaven and a new earth (*1 Enoch* 45:4f.; 91:16), of a new creation (*1 Enoch* 72:1). This present world is full of evil and hopeless. The apocalyptists abandoned it. But they seized firmly on the new age, which they saw as in sharp contrast, and they continually bring out the blessedness and glory that are characteristics of it.

R. Meyer is another who sees the two ages doctrine of apocalyptic as important. Indeed he thinks that in this respect apocalyptic has made a permanent contribution. He sees the roots of apocalyptic as 'for the most part outside Israel, namely, in Iran and the East Mediterranean world'. Thus he can refer to 'true apocalyptic of Iranian origin' that, he maintains, 'offers "disclosures" about the rise and fall and change of world epochs. Adopted by Judaism in the Persian-Hell. period and integrated into its own view of history, the doctrine of epochs finally led to the idea of two world epochs, which was destined to outlast apocalyptic and to become an enduring principle of faith.'[6] There is room for argument about his view of origins. As we have already seen, some highly competent scholars have argued for an origin within Judaism, and I do not see how their arguments can be resisted. But Meyer's point about the 'enduring principle of faith' is well taken. To this day we are indebted to the apocalyptists for making this point so firmly that it has become an integral part of subsequent religion.

Not all of this, of course, is present in every sample of apocalyptic. But the trend towards dualism is characteristic of apocalyptic as a whole. As we have already noticed, this is often explained as due to the influence of Persian literature and there may be something in the contention. Certainly some of the ideas of the apocalyptists have a marked resemblance to certain Persian ideas. But it is also possible that we have here a development of trends already present in Old Testament teaching. Thus G. E. Ladd points out that in the Old Testament we have ideas like that of a redeemed earth

---

[6] R. Meyer, in *Theological Dictionary of the New Testament*, ed. G. Friedrich, trans. G. W. Bromiley, vi, Grand Rapids, 1968, p. 827.

(Is. 32:15–18; 11:6–9; 65:17; 66:22), and of the divine visitation (Is. 13:13; 34:4; 51:6; Hg. 2:7).[7]

He makes the further point that some Old Testament passages speak of a new order rather like this present earth, whereas others refer to a new heaven and a new earth. Sometimes apocalyptists put the two together. They can speak of a temporal kingdom and see it as followed by an eternal kingdom in a new order (4 Ezra 7:28f.).

C. C. Torrey, writing about apocalyptic in general and not dualism in particular, holds that this kind of literature 'certainly assimilated, from the beginning, more or less foreign material; but in its essential features it seems to have been truly Jewish in its origin, as it continued to be in its subsequent history'.[8] This does seem to be the true position. Apocalyptic was basically Jewish. It had deep roots in the religion of the Old Testament. We saw in an earlier section that during the period when it flourished a multitude of ideas, Iranian and Hellenistic and other, flooded into Palestine. Jewish writers could and did take what suited them from these ideas. But this did not mean that they were abandoning their essential position. They were not. The writers of apocalyptic used what was foreign to emphasize what was Jewish.

We should also be clear that apocalyptic dualism is always seen within the framework of a basic monotheism. This is plain enough where it is a question of this world and the world to come, but it is also the case when Satan or other evil spirits are referred to. These have no independent existence. Their activities are confined to the area determined by God. There is a real dualism, but it is never absolute.

Pseudonymity

The apocalypses tend to be pseudonymous. As we have already seen, the writers of this class of literature did not usually claim direct inspiration like the prophets. They did

---

[7] G. E. Ladd, in *Baker's Dictionary of Theology*, p. 52.
[8] C. C. Torrey, in *The Jewish Encyclopedia*, i, p. 672.

not apparently feel themselves as directly moved by God. And in any case, by their time men seem to have been agreed that the prophetic canon had closed. The prophetic literature was a definite, known group of books of divine origin, and nothing could any longer be added to it. Prophecy was held in the very highest esteem, but it had ceased.

R. H. Charles sees the closing of the canon as the reason for the pseudonymity. When the Law was raised to the highest place and the prophetic canon was closed, there was no obvious way for a new writer to get a hearing. The way the apocalyptist chose was to attribute his work to an illustrious ancient. Charles thinks that things were different among the Christians. They had a new belief in the reality of prophecy. They saw prophets operating in their very midst, so did not regard prophecy as having ceased. For a long time there was no closed New Testament canon. Thus Paul (2 Thes. 2 and 1 Cor. 15) and John, he thinks, wrote apocalypses under their own names.[9]

But Charles may here be claiming too much. There seems no reason why the apocalyptists should not have gained some sort of hearing even after the canon was closed. After all, other types of literature flourished without being pseudonymous. Yet the closed canon was probably one factor in the situation. No recent upstart could be numbered in the goodly fellowship of the prophets. What, then, was a new speaker to do when he wanted a hearing? He could not qualify for membership in a band which was already closed, and he lived in a day when what was ancient was held in the highest esteem. One way of attracting attention was to enlist the support of the ancients (an early example of 'If you can't lick 'em, join 'em'!). While his contemporaries might be ready to treat lightly a writing emanating from their own day and their own circle, it might be different with some great teacher of the past. Thus the new writer might see his revelations as given originally to Ezra or Moses or Abraham or Baruch or some other recognized hero of the faith.

How far this pseudonymity concealed the real authorship

[9] R. H. Charles, *Religious Development Between the Old and the New Testaments*, London, 1914, pp. 38–46.

of a writing from contemporaries we do not know, but the device was certainly adopted by the apocalyptists with some regularity. At the least it gave an authoritative ring to what was said. And where the ascription was taken seriously, it must have added immensely to the respect accorded the writings. To have a writing bearing the honoured name of Moses, for example, which foretold events between Moses' day and that of the reader, events which could be checked and which had in fact occurred just as 'predicted', must have been a great consolation to the troubled in their days of difficulty. The accuracy of events up till that time would give confidence that the document could be trusted in other matters.

It is not unlikely also that the apocalyptist felt that he was saying the kind of things the great one of the past would have said had he been confronted with the contemporary situation. Sometimes at least he seems to have identified himself with the hero whose spokesman he was. In this, apocalyptic contrasts with prophecy. The prophet stood forth boldly as he was and spoke in the name of his God. His person was important, for his hearers would know that it was Isaiah or Jeremiah or whoever, who thus spoke for God. But the person of the apocalyptist was suppressed. He did not stand forth like the prophet but merged himself with the past hero whose words he purported to give.

A further consideration which may have been important is that the content of the apocalypse seems often to be related to the character of the seer chosen as the hero. Thus Russell points out that *Jubilees*, concerned as it is with the high place of the Law and the priesthood, is fittingly linked with the name of Moses. The cosmopolitan *1 Enoch* is associated with the ancient who was the great-great-grandfather of Ham and Japhet as well as of Shem and who may well be thought of as 'the supreme cosmopolitan of antiquity'. *2 Esdras* is just as fittingly linked with Ezra, whose ardent nationalism accords with an author for whom 'God was the God of Israel rather than of all mankind'.[1] The content of the apocalypse might

[1] D. S. Russell, *The Method and Message of Jewish Apocalyptic*, pp. 138f.

be such that its author thought that it ought to be associated with a specific person from antiquity.

Some feel that the pseudonymity of the apocalypses is connected with their message. The authors of these books were not writing about mundane matters of the kind of which any man might be expected to have knowledge. They were concerned with another world, and there was thus a peculiar fitness about having the message come from a being who belonged to that world. L. H. Brockington puts it this way:

> ... the message of the apocalyptists was one that showed knowledge not only of this world but of a world beyond this – beyond it both in time and in space – the world of God. None but a denizen of that world would be capable of speaking with authority about it.[2]

About twenty different names were used as far as our present information goes and each is outstanding for one reason or another. Enoch seems to have had a special attraction, perhaps because of his dramatic removal from the earthly scene.

We should perhaps notice that the two books in the Bible that are most commonly classed as apocalyptic, namely, Daniel and Revelation, are exceptions at least in this respect. Daniel is often claimed as an ancient hero, but this is asserted, not proved.[3] Apart from this book, we have no real evidence for the existence of a sixth-century BC Daniel active in Babylon (or for that matter anywhere else). On the evidence so far known to us there is no attempt here at fathering a book on to an illustrious predecessor. And Revelation tells us in the opening verse that it came from John. Whether we equate this John with the son of Zebedee or whether we regard him as quite distinct, in either case the writing is not pseudonymous. It tells us the author's name right at the beginning. And he is not a past hero.

[2] L. H. Brockington, in *Journal of Theological Studies*, n.s., iv, 1953, p. 19.
[3] See below, pp. 76ff.

A literary form

We should understand apocalyptic as a literary device, a way of getting the message across. It set forth the teaching of the author, but it did not give a description of something that actually happened. In this there is a contrast with prophecy. The prophets had a profound sense of communion with God and they told people what happened when they were close to God. They felt that God spoke to them and gave them messages for His people. They saw visions and related them. Modern scholars often feel that they themselves would describe what happened in terms other than those used by the prophets. But they would not deny that the prophets are referring to genuine psychological states and happenings. They are not engaging in pious fiction and inventing the revelation.

Perhaps 'pious fiction' is a little hard as a description of apocalyptic. But no-one takes seriously the idea that when an apocalyptist speaks of certain revelations as made, say, to Baruch, he is describing what actually happened to Baruch, or, for that matter, what actually happened to himself. He is using a literary device to convey a message, not describing events of the past. He may well feel that what he says Baruch (or whoever his hero is) saw and heard were the kind of things that Baruch was likely to have seen and heard. But in the last resort his attribution of these things to Baruch is imaginative. It is not, and is not meant to be, factual.

This is not to deny that on occasion apocalyptists may have had genuine psychological experiences which are reflected in their writings. Most critics, for example, would see such experiences behind *4 Ezra*. We noted earlier that even when conventional imagery is employed, the writer may on occasion be recording personal experiences of his own. If an apocalyptist has genuine experiences there is no reason why he should not incorporate them in his writing. The fact that he has had these experiences may well strengthen his conviction of the propriety of attributing them to his spokesman. But this is not a necessary understanding of his writings.

Basically what he is doing is adopting a certain literary convention and framing his message in accordance with it.

This means that there is a certain stress on writing among the apocalyptists. In this they contrast with both the prophets and the Rabbis. The prophetic books appear to record sermons and the like uttered by the prophets. While there is no reason to doubt that they wrote some things, and even that they wrote some things originally, most of their ministry seems to have been concerned with the spoken word. They were preachers first of all. Their prophecies for the most part seem to have been spoken at the first and only afterwards written down.

The Rabbis also seem to have emphasized oral tradition. For a long time they passed on their voluminous teachings solely by word of mouth. In time the sheer bulk of this tradition became so great that no one man could know it all by heart. It simply had to be written down if it were not to perish. But until that day came, the Rabbis seem to have felt that if a man had to look a thing up in a book he did not know it. Any scholar worth his salt would know whole books by heart, and there are some prodigious feats of memory on record.

But the apocalyptists put great faith in the written word. There is no evidence that they preferred teaching by word of mouth. This does not mean that they did not use oral tradition. Most scholars agree that the apocalyptists often made use of traditional material, particularly when a given writing is associated with a figure like Enoch or Ezra around whom many traditions clustered. Such traditions may well have been carried on by word of mouth. But this is not the characteristic method of apocalyptic. Rather, the evidence is that the apocalyptists had something to say and chose to write it down. For them the written page was an eminently suitable medium. They were literary men, and saw their compositions as powerful means of propagating their teaching. From the first their message was written.

Rewritten history

A feature of many apocalypses is that they take past history and rewrite it in the form of prophecy. Thus in *1 Enoch* 85–90 there is a summary of history from the time of Adam until the coming of Messiah. From the standpoint of the historical Enoch most of this would, of course, have been future, and it thus appears to be prophecy. The writer of *4 Ezra* locates himself in the historical process with some precision: 'For the world-age is divided into twelve parts; nine (parts) of it are passed already, and the half of the tenth part; and there remain of it two (parts), besides the half of the tenth part' (*4 Ezra* 14:11f.). Sometimes the writer gives a survey of the whole history of the world; sometimes he starts with the time of the reputed author and works forward.

In view of the normal apocalyptic pessimism about the present it is interesting to notice that there is a very different attitude to the past. There God has acted. It is curious that the apocalyptist did not draw the conclusion that the God who had acted in history before could do so again. But He did not. He combined a firm faith in a God who acted of old with an equally firm conviction that there was now no hope for the world until the catastrophic intervention at the End.

When the apocalyptist goes on to conjecture the form of happenings still future in his own day, his forecasts have a habit of being less precise than those of past history. Moreover, they are not likely to be as exact in their fulfilment. This gives scholars a clue to the dating of such writings. They assume that the apocalyptist will have clear and good knowledge of history up to his own day, and especially of that just before his own day. But he will not know with certainty what is about to happen and there will be a difference in the way he deals with the two periods. When this is so, it is clear that we are able to give a fairly precise date for the writing.

An interesting feature of this rewritten history is that there is a tendency to concentrate on events. Usually (though not invariably) the apocalyptists do not name people but describe them, leaving it to their readers to identify the people from the descriptions. If they do use names (for example, 'Chittim'), these are not the accepted names of any people as far as is known. Unfortunately we usually do not know what the meaning of such names is, and often there is dispute as to which people are in mind.

Ethical teaching

It is usually held that the apocalyptists are not as forthright as the prophets in their ethical teaching. It is not for them the major interest as it is for the prophets. Typically the prophet is a stern critic who denounces the men of his day and calls on them to repent. Now and then he does produce passages of comfort, but these are not typical. Many critics, for example, regard the last half-chapter of Amos as un-authentic on the grounds that such a comfortable passage is out of place. Amos denounces. He does not console. Whatever be the truth about this particular section of the prophecy, the general position is clear. The prophets are much more likely to be found denouncing sinners than comforting saints.

Not so the apocalyptists. Typically they were interested in consoling and sustaining the righteous remnant rather than in castigating the nominally religious. Where the prophets were concerned with the question of why those called to be the people of God should live such evil lives, the apocalyptists were facing the problem of why the righteous should be called upon to undergo such sufferings. Their aim accordingly was to strengthen and comfort those whom they saw as serving God. They aimed to confirm them in their right ways, not to reform them. They held out before them the prospect of ultimate vindication coupled with the complete overthrow of their oppressors.

This contrast should not be drawn too sharply. That the prophets are capable of warm consolation as well as of stern denunciation is clear. We need look no further than Isaiah 40ff. for ample proof, and comforting passages are available in other prophecies as well. From the opposite side some object to the limitation of ethical teaching in the apocalypses.

Thus R. H. Charles can say, 'apocalyptic no less than pro-phecy is radically ethical',[4] and again,

> ... apocalyptic was essentially ethical. In every crisis of the world's history, when the good cause was overthrown and the wrong triumphant, its insistent demand was ever: 'Shall not the Judge of all the earth do right?' and its uncompro-mising optimism, its unconquerable faith under the most overwhelming disasters was: 'God reigns, and righteousness shall ultimately prevail.'[5]

But with all respect this scarcely meets the objection. That the apocalyptists were whole-heartedly committed to the cause of right is not in question. Nor is their profound convic-tion that right will ultimately prevail. These things are clear. The point at issue is whether the original readers of apocalyp-tic were being comforted and confirmed in their way of life or denounced and urged to repent.

That the apocalyptists were basically seeking to console and strengthen their readers should, I think, be maintained even in the face of the fact that sometimes the apocalypses do contain notable ethical statements. This latter point should not be overlooked. It is not true to say that there is no ethical teaching in these writings. The apocalyptists looked for up-right conduct and on occasion they can inculcate the demand for social justice quite in the prophetic manner (cf. *Testament of Benjamin* 10:3). Indeed, it can be said that a serious ethical purpose is implied in all they write. The hope they held out at the End was for the righteous, not for all men. And while they fix their gaze on the End, they do not await it idly with no concern for morality. They are anxious that men do the right. Indeed, on occasion the very nearness of the End adds a note of urgency to their ethical concern. If the Judge of all mankind is about to make His appearance, men cannot put off repentance and amendment of life. They must do it now.

But when all this is said the ethical imperative is not characteristic of them as it is of the prophets. In the last resort their interest is in eschatology, not ethics.

[4] R. H. Charles, *The Apocrypha and Pseudepigrapha of the Old Testa-ment*, ii, p. 16.
[5] *Ibid.*, p. 30.

Sometimes when they do engage in ethical teaching it turns out to be other than the kind of thing we see in the prophets. For example, in *1 Enoch* we find some forthright denunciations of evil such as, 'But ye – ye have not been steadfast, nor done the commandments of the Lord, but ye have turned away and spoken proud and hard words. . . .' This is the kind of denunciation so typical of the prophets and we feel that we are on familiar ground. But after some lines of this kind of thing we come to the contrast: 'and there shall be forgiveness of sins, and every mercy and peace and forbearance: there shall be salvation unto them, a goodly light. And for all of you sinners there shall be no salvation, but on you all shall abide a curse' (*1 Enoch* 5:4–6). Plainly this is not the prophetic denunciation of a sinning people. It is a division of mankind into the sinners who will be accursed and the elect who will receive blessing.

Typically, then, the urgent thing for the apocalyptist is to bring cheer and comfort to the righteous. God's people are being troubled by the wicked and it is important that they be given the help that will enable them to come through the trial without wavering. The writer encourages them for the conflict. He tries to give them the firm assurance that God is supreme and that He will infallibly bring His purpose to pass in His own good time. A. C. Welch reminds us that we ourselves know something of the 'comfort' aspect of apocalyptic by referring us to the New Testament book of Revelation:

> . . . it is to a New Testament Apocalypse that we owe those great, grave utterances which have passed into the perennial use of the Church in the presence of death, and which have consoled more troubled hearts than any other words in literature. John bewilders his readers, as he passes from his crashing trumpets and streaming bowls to describe the red dragon which vomited a flood out of its mouth, but he has comforted the Church in all its mourning generations and has been able to turn its sorrow into triumph. The mighty music of his unforced sentences comes back to stay up the hearts of men, when they are most intimately threatened with defeat. When a man could write: 'They

shall hunger no more neither thirst any more, neither shall the sun light on them nor any heat, for the Lamb which is in the midst of the throne shall feed them and shall lead them unto living fountains of water, and God shall wipe away all tears from their eyes,' it is idle to represent him as aloof from the needs and aspirations of men, nor can anything else he writes be readily pronounced negligible.[6]

Prediction

Sometimes people deal with something very like this point in a different way. It is asserted that for the prophet the important thing is preaching rather than prediction, whereas for the apocalyptist what matters is prediction and not preaching. But this antithesis is too sharp. Indeed, A. C. Welch roundly denies a distinction along these lines. He says:

> . . . it is idle to urge that the prophets were essentially preachers, while the apocalyptists wrote down their visions, for Ezekiel combined both methods and Jeremiah wrote a letter to his co-religionists in Babylon . . . the essential features of the two forms of thought and action remained the same. Apocalypse and prophecy hold the same conceptions of God and of His relations to the world, and both sought to say what God, being what He was, must effect when He revealed His will in a world which had forgotten its dependence on Him.[7]

But this scarcely grapples with the main point. While there is no doubt that the prophets and the apocalyptists held many ideas in common, it is another thing altogether to assert that there is no significant difference in their respective approaches. The prophets were indeed concerned to preach, and the apocalyptists to predict, and the reverse is true also. But it is a question of balance and of outlook. H. H. Rowley recognizes that both are concerned with the future. He rejects

[6] A. C. Welch, *Visions of the End,* London, n.d., pp. 16f.
[7] *Ibid.,* p. 32.

the view of Charles that 'Prediction is not in any sense an essential of prophecy', preferring that of A. S. Peake,

> It is rather unfortunate that the reaction from the old-fashioned view that prophecy was in the main prediction has led to the prevalent belief that the prophets were scarcely concerned with the future at all. . . . For really the predictive element in prophecy was very prominent.[8]

He gives his own view about the difference between the prophets and the apocalyptists on this point in these words: 'Speaking generally, the prophets foretold the future that should arise out of the present, while the apocalyptists foretold the future that should break into the present.'[9]

There is certainly a sense in which the prophets preached, but this was linked with their confidence in what God would do in the future and so with their predictions. And, as Rowley says, they were concerned with the future that would arise out of the present. Present situations would be resolved and present sins would be punished. They spoke as preachers concerned with the shortcomings of their congregations. They directed men to the will of God for them and called on them to repent. God had always been active in history and He would continue to be active. So they proclaim what God would do just as powerfully as what He had done. Prediction was part of their method. It was not to be used on every occasion, but it was always there as a possibility. The ability to predict was so much a mark of the true prophet that Israel was invited to use it as a test. A false prophet could be known by the failure of his predictions (Dt. 18:22). By contrast the Lord would do nothing without revealing His secret to His servants the prophets (Am. 3:7).

The apocalyptists had their eyes fixed on a more remote future. They were interested in the way God would break into this world of time and sense and bring an end to this whole present system. They were carrying on the prophetic system, for as Russell puts it,

---

[8] H. H. Rowley, *The Relevance of Apocalyptic*, p. 38, n. 1.
[9] *Ibid.*, p. 38.

... for the most part the apocalyptists were prophetic voices who believed that the time spoken of beforehand had now come and that ancient prophecy was on the point of being realized in a manner beyond the understanding of the prophets themselves and of the rank and file of men in their own day.[1]

While much is held in common there is certainly a difference in emphasis.

Historical perspective

We might put our next point by saying that the apocalyptists were more interested in theology than in history. Of course, in a sense this is true of the prophets also. First and foremost the prophets were men of God. But there is a contrast as well as a resemblance, for the prophets also took history very seriously. They looked for God's purposes to be worked out within the historical process and they earnestly set themselves to the task of directing the nation and its leaders into right action in the here and now so that important historical consequences might follow. All they did was in the light of the kingdom of God that they saw on the horizon, but meantime they addressed themselves to the problems of their day. As Ladd puts it, for them 'Historical judgments are seen as realized eschatology'.[2]

The apocalyptists do not see history this way. There is a sense in which they took history very seriously, and some scholars have pointed out that, more than any others up till their time, the apocalyptists saw history as a unity. One great purpose of God was being worked out in the affairs of men, so that all history, past, present and future, was bound up together. History became the theatre of God's operations. Thus, Amos N. Wilder can say, apocalyptic

> spoke to its own historical situation and the existing sense of reality. It pioneered the first universal view of history

[1] D. S. Russell, *The Method and Message of Jewish Apocalyptic*, p. 100.
[2] G. E. Ladd, in *Baker's Dictionary of Theology*, p. 52.

including all peoples and all times. It took history with utter seriousness, confronting the seemingly total disaster of the present and assigning meaning and hope to it in terms of the wider cosmic drama.[3]

The thought that apocalyptic takes history with full seriousness has, of course, been argued strongly by Wolfhart Pannenberg. Thus he says,

> In those prophetic circles which were the starting point of the Apocalyptic movement the whole history of Israel and of the world into the far future was understood for the first time as a continuing totality of Divine activity realizing a plan which had been decided at the beginning of creation. Accordingly, God's final revelation, the revelation of His glory, together with the glorification of the righteous was now hoped for as the End of all occurrence.[4]

Gerhard Gloege is another who stresses the importance of the apocalyptists for an understanding of history. He outlines views on world history he sees reflected in the book of Daniel and proceeds,

> It is impossible to understand world-history without paying attention to its three zones, 'beginning, middle and end'. Three motives are at work in it: God's eternal plan is its source; the temporal conflict between human and divine power extends over its course; and God's eternal kingdom is its destination.[5]

He sees all this as of continuing significance, for later he says,

> The Christian world has taken over this understanding of history which was given its distinctive content in the New Testament. The historical consciousness of the West, from Augustine to Hegel and beyond to our own day, has been largely due to the impulse of sublime apocalyptic. Recent historical knowledge bears the stamp of its thought-forms; it has preserved the outlines of what was at that time a

[3] A. N. Wilder, in *Interpretation*, xxv, 1971, p. 443.

[4] W. Pannenberg, in *Interpretation*, xxi, 1967, p. 168, n. 4.

[5] G. Gloege, *The Day of His Coming*, p. 55.

new style of question, while subjecting it to a critical and methodical examination.[6]

Such writers as these insist that the apocalyptists saw more clearly than others a great divine purpose being worked out from the beginning of creation to the end of time. It is a grand conception.

But it cannot be held without reservation that this was characteristic of the apocalyptic outlook. William R. Murdock reminds us that we must not forget the typical dualism of the apocalypses. The apocalyptists were quite sure that there is evil in the world, opposed to God and opposed by God. 'For apocalypticism, history was the sphere of conflict between the divine and the demonic wills, and all that had made history a problem for the Jews was attributed to the demonic will.'[7] But if history is the sphere in which there is a mighty conflict between God and the forces of evil it is not easy to see it as the working out of the divine plan. Evil has to be taken seriously in its own right. Murdock sees history in the view of the apocalyptists as 'in part the expression of the demonic will'.[8] If we take apocalyptic dualism seriously, it is hard to see how this conclusion is to be resisted.

We should notice further that the apocalyptists did not really see revelation as taking place in history. We do not find them drawing men's attention to contemporary events in which the hand of God is to be discerned. God, for them, reveals Himself in apocalyptic literature rather than in history. They often picture their writings as uttered by some great one of antiquity, but kept hidden until their own day. In all the intervening years men could not know God's purpose. Now that the apocalypse has appeared they can know it. To cite Murdock again,

For the apocalyptists, however, the present revelation was not a historical revelation (i.e. a revelation in the public

[6] *Ibid.*, p. 58.
[7] W. R. Murdock, in *Interpretation*, xxi, 1967, p. 174. Murdock sees the theological implication of certain apocalyptic statements in this way: '. . . monotheism has given way to dualism' (*ibid.*).
[8] *Ibid.*, p. 180.

c

and concrete events of world history), as Wilckens supposes, but a literary revelation (i.e. a revelation that is to be found in the apocalypses).[9]

The apocalyptic certainty that God acted in the days of the saints of old coupled with an equal certainty that He will intervene spectacularly at the end and overthrow all evil does not mean that God is working in history now in the way the prophets saw Him working.

It is difficult to maintain that the apocalyptists took history seriously in the way the great prophets did.[1] Hanson insists: 'In dealing with Jewish apocalyptic we must speak of abdication of responsibility to the historical realm, and not the collapse of the notion of the historical.'[2] But he contrasts the way the prophets used history with that employed by the apocalyptists:

> In classical prophecy the realm of human history was the realm within which the covenant relationship between Yahweh and his people was being carried out; historical events were carriers of cosmic significance.

But in apocalyptic (he is speaking specifically of Daniel),

> History is used as a timetable indicating how close men are to the ultimate event which would break the power which the inimical powers hold on the elect. The dynamic of a history which is the living out of a genuine covenant relationship yields to the inflexibility of a history which becomes a timetable of cosmic events: 'for what is determined shall be done' (11:36).[3]

[9] *Ibid.*, p. 186. Again he says that 'the eschaton was understood in apocalypticism not as the goal of history, but as the impingement of eternity that destroys history; and the eschatological revelation was understood, not as the sum of all historical revelations, but as the *doxa* of God bursting in upon this aeon of darkness from the aeon of light' (*ibid.*, p. 187).

[1] G. Ebeling thinks that apocalyptic 'is a mythological interpretation of history and as such has in fact the dangerous tendency to construct history and to deal wholesale with it in a highly abstract way – in other words, actually to escape from history' (*Journal for Theology and the Church*, no. 6, 1969, p. 64).

[2] P. D. Hanson, in *Interpretation*, xxv, 1971, p. 478, n. 19.

[3] *Ibid.*, pp. 478f.

It is not true to say that the apocalyptists have no interest in history. But they do use it in a way quite different from that of the prophets.

By contrast with the prophets Ladd thinks that the apocalyptists have 'lost this tension between history and eschatology'.[4] Von Rad is even more definite:

> The decisive factor, as I see it, is the incompatibility between apocalyptic literature's view of history and that of the prophets. The prophetic message is specifically rooted in the saving history, that is to say, it is rooted in definite election traditions. But there is no way which leads from this to the apocalyptic view of history.[5]

It would be true to say that for the most part the apocalyptists are content to abandon the present and look for the future consummation. They are sure of the final outcome. But they do not see it as other than a divine breaking in on this present historical process. The historical process itself they are ready to abandon.

[4] G. E. Ladd, in *Baker's Dictionary of Theology*, loc. cit.
[5] G. von Rad, *Old Testament Theology*, ii, p. 303. Again he says, '. . . we may even ask whether apocalyptic literature had any existential relationship with history at all' (*ibid.*, p. 304). Wilder notes Koch, Hengel, and Schmidt as scholars who differ from von Rad (*Interpretation*, xxv, 1971, p. 443). But, while his citations perhaps show that von Rad's position is overstated, they do not show that the apocalyptists' view of history was anything like that of the prophets.

APOCALYPTIC AND LAW

There is something of a contrast between the apocalyptic approach and that of the Rabbis. Judaism as a whole tended to put its emphasis on the Law. This had been given by Moses and it was the high point of revelation. Everything must be seen in its light. Actually in this respect there is not much difference between the two, for the apocalyptists just as much as the Rabbis saw the Law as a God-given treasure. They esteemed and extolled it. *1 Enoch* regards the Law as 'eternal' and pronounces a 'Woe!' on those who transgress it (*1 Enoch* 99:2; *cf.* 5:4; 99:14). The apocalyptists saw it as their guide to conduct as well as the centre of revelation. In fact they seem to have tied the origin of their kind of literature to the same fountainhead as that of the Law. In *2 Esdras* 14 it is presupposed that scripture has all been lost, '. . . thy law has been burned, and so no one knows the things which have been done or will be done by thee' (v. 21). Ezra asks God to send the Holy Spirit into him so that he may write 'the things which were written in thy law, that men may be able to find the path, and that those who wish to live in the last days may live' (v. 22). God granted the prayer and for forty days Ezra dictated solidly to five fast writers. In this way ninety-four books were produced. Ezra was commanded to make public twenty-four of them, which are plainly the Old Testament.[1] It is sometimes said that the other seventy books represent the oral law, but this seems unlikely as Ezra is to keep them secret (*cf.* vv. 6, 26), 'in order to give them to the

[1] G. H. Box comments, 'The number 24 is the ordinary reckoning of the O.T. books (5+8+11). In the Talmud and Midrash the O.T. is regularly termed "the twenty-four holy Scriptures" ' (*The Apocrypha and Pseudepigrapha of the Old Testament*, ed. R. H. Charles, ii, Oxford, 1963, p. 624).

wise among your people' (v. 46). This seems to refer to the
apocalyptic books, books which were not for the ordinary
man but for 'the wise'. Seen in this way apocalyptic and the
Law are in no contradiction. They have a common origin
and are to be seen together. Dietrich Rössler's 'decisive principle of apocalyptic' is relevant here:

> The significance of the law in apocalyptic lies in the fact
> that it preserves to the individual his place in the people of
> God, that in this way he remains a member of the chosen
> community and is led towards salvation with the rest.[2]

Seen in this way the Law fits very naturally into the apocalyptic scheme of things and there is no disharmony.

But the development of the Rabbinic system did not see
things in quite this way. The Rabbis made the study of the
Law their most important occupation, and they elevated the
Law as the one authoritative deposit of revelation to the
supreme place in their way of life. Despite the help given by
the rise of oral tradition, it may not unfairly be said that they
saw the Law as a static deposit of truth. It was unchanging.
It stood as a constant to which appeal could always be made.

By contrast there was a freshness about apocalyptic. While
not minimizing the place of the Law, it yet put stress on
revelation made in visions and the like and adapted to the
current situation. Wherever men stressed immediate experience they were out of harmony with the basic tenet of Rabbinism. The Rabbis were essentially backward looking, the
apocalyptists forward looking. The Rabbis could not come
to terms with the apocalyptic view of life. It is significant that
the apocalypses were preserved for the most part not by
Judaism but by Christianity. Those apocalypses which made
no appeal to the Christians have usually perished. For a time
Christians produced apocalypses of their own (e.g. Hermas),
but presently they, too, ceased. Apocalyptic remains for the
most part a Jewish phenomenon, but it was produced by a
segment of Judaism with an outlook uncongenial to Rabbinism. It is now apparent that first-century Judaism was far

---

[2] Cited by G. Ebeling, in *Journal for Theology and the Church*, no. 6,
1969, p. 50, n. 5.

from monolithic. There were many cross-currents. The eventual triumph of Pharisaism, with its corollary that the writings of other schools of thought ceased to be copied, have hidden this from us, at least in a measure.

One of the most important things about the Qumran scrolls is that they let us see a sect of Judaism other than Pharisaism through its own eyes and not those of its enemies. The writings of the apocalyptists in a measure render us the same service. They show us an outlook that emphasized experience and novelty. There is something attractive about this view that sought to breathe new life into Judaism by stressing that God had not ceased to speak to His people nor to act on their behalf.

R. H. Charles connects this with pseudonymity. He says,

> The Law which claimed to be the highest and final word from God could tolerate no fresh message from God, and so, when men were moved by the Spirit of God to make known their visions relating to the past, the present, and the future, and to proclaim the higher ethical truths they had won, they could not do so openly, but were forced to resort to pseudonymous publication.[3]

For our present discussion the significant point is not his view on pseudonymity but his recognition of the incompatibility between the Rabbinic approach and that of the apocalyptists. The Law 'could tolerate no fresh message from God'. Of course there is nothing in the Law itself that prevents fresh revelation, as the writings of the prophets and the whole of the New Testament make plain. Again, we have already noticed that the apocalyptists honoured and obeyed the Law. But the Rabbinic understanding of the Law was an intolerant one. The Rabbis could find no room for the claims of apocalyptic. They were too rigid in their understanding of the meaning of the Law to take kindly to a movement that stressed new revelations.

[3] R. H. Charles, *The Apocrypha and Pseudepigrapha of the Old Testament*, ii, p. 163.

APOCALYPTIC AND WISDOM

A point which is often overlooked in discussion of apocalyptic is its connection with the Wisdom literature. This is literature of the kind we see in the Bible in Proverbs and Ecclesiastes, and which flourished in a number of countries in antiquity. There are some notable examples from Egypt, for instance. It often featured short, pithy aphorisms of the kind we see in Proverbs, but it could also issue in longer and more sustained treatments of themes.[1] While it was basically concerned with how to live happily in the human family, it could cover a wide range of topics. The Wisdom books were the writings of men of culture with a profound interest in the world in which they lived. Their interests ranged over a wide field, including much that we would include under the heading 'science' as well as the studies we assign to the humanities.

Sometimes there is explicit connection between apocalyptic and wisdom. Thus Daniel was given the kind of instruction that was typical of the wise men of Babylon (Dn. 1:3ff.), and in due course he found himself 'chief prefect over all the wise men of Babylon' (Dn. 2:48). Wisdom was prominent among his virtues (Dn. 5:11). Again, Enoch speaks of certain things it were better to declare only to the men of old, 'but even from those that come after we will not withhold the beginning of wisdom'. He modestly adds, 'Till the present day such wisdom has never been given by the Lord of Spirits as I have received according to my insight' (*1 Enoch* 37:3f.).

In keeping with this, some of the topics discussed by the apocalyptists are the kind of thing we see in the Wisdom literature. Thus von Rad finds 'an enormous accumulation of

[1] See the article, 'Wisdom Literature' by D. A. Hubbard, in *The New Bible Dictionary*, ed. J. D. Douglas *et al.*, London, 1962.

knowledge' in the *Apocalypse of Enoch* 'about the development of civilisation (Enoch VIII), the heavenly bodies (Enoch LXXII–LXXIX), the calendar, meteorology, and geography'.[2] And what is true of Enoch is true of a number of other apocalyptic writings. Betz refers to 'the strong interest the apocalyptist has in "knowledge" and "science" (for example, cosmology, astrology, demonology, botany, zoology, pharmacy, and so forth)'.[3] It would be true to say that the writers of this class of literature have an interest in and an acquaintance with the kind of topic that was often treated by the Wisdom writers. Von Rad goes so far as to say that Wisdom is 'the real matrix from which apocalyptic literature originates'.[4] He has not been able to persuade very many that this is in fact the case. The differences present a difficult problem from this point of view. For example, the Wisdom literature lacks the eschatological interest that is such a dominant feature of apocalypse. Where Wisdom is basically concerned with this world, apocalyptic stresses the next. There are other not inconsiderable differences also. But the points of contact are interesting, and the connection between the two groups of writings should not be overlooked. There are certainly some affinities.

[2] G. von Rad, *Old Testament Theology*, ii, p. 306.
[3] H. D. Betz, in *Journal for Theology and the Church*, no. 6, 1969, p. 136.
[4] G. von Rad, *op. cit.*, p. 306.

IRRESPONSIBILITY OF
THE APOCALYPTISTS

One feature of apocalyptic that we must not overlook is the fact that it represents the opinions and suggestions of men without power. Its authors could put forward their ideas with confidence, secure in the knowledge that they would not have to undergo the sharp test of seeing how they would work in practice. In this respect the difference between them and the prophets is not unlike that between the government and the opposition. The party in power must take a good deal of care over its solutions to current problems, for it will proceed to put them into effect and take the consequences. The party will be held responsible should the result be unfortunate. By contrast, the opposition can engage in the luxury of less guarded speculation. It knows its solutions will not be put to the hard test of how they will work out.

We may liken the prophets to the party that forms the government. They were sometimes the trusted advisers of those in power, as, for example, was Isaiah. Even where this was not the case, the prophet was putting forward a solution that might well be taken seriously and which he hoped would be.

Not so the apocalyptist. He knew that the foreign overlord would reject anything he said, and he could accordingly indulge in the wildest speculation. He would never be proved wrong by having his advice followed with disastrous consequences. In any case he had written off this world and its activities, so there was no question of his trying seriously to provide workable solutions to its problems.

E. F. Scott expresses it like this:

> The prophets belonged to a free nation, of which they were the trusted advisers. They lived in times of terrible emergency, when the fate of the nation depended on their

counsel, and they could not venture to speak lightly. The apocalypses come from a time when Israel was subject to foreign powers. Their authors are free to indulge their own fancies and to offer conjectures and speculations, knowing that they stand safely apart from the actual direction of events. Between them and the prophets there is much the same kind of difference as between the political doctrinaire and the responsible statesman.[1]

This is not to discredit the apocalypses. Their writers were men with serious purpose and they had something important to say to the men of their day. But in this matter of workable political solutions they had little to contribute. They put no faith in the political systems they saw and they made no really serious suggestions for an alternative.

[1] E. F. Scott, *The Book of Revelation*, London, 1939, p. 12.

APOCALYPTIC AND
THE OLD TESTAMENT

Almost all would agree that there is apocalyptic in the Old Testament, the only disagreement being as to its extent. Some see it but rarely, others see it in many places. Thus S. B. Frost finds it almost throughout the prophets. He envisages a time after the exile 'when the apocalyptic type of mind found an opportunity for self-expression, not in the writing or compilation of books, but in the interpreting of earlier oracles and in making that interpretation clear to all by an extensive "glossing" '.[1] This enables him to find apocalyptic very widely, either as original or as due to the work of glossators. As an example, he sees the book of Isaiah as extensively worked over by apocalyptists. Originally there were three main booklets, 2:6–10, 13–23, 28–31.

> To each of these booklets a 'fabricated apocalypse' has been added before the three were put together: thus 2⁶–10 receives 11–12, 13–23 receives 24–7, and 28–31 receives 32–3. When these three booklets were put together the resulting collection received as a whole a further apocalyptic addition, 34–5. We are thus presented with four such 'fabricated apocalypses'.[2]

Such views have not commended themselves widely. There is a strong subjective element involved and most scholars have not been able to see apocalyptic (as distinct from eschatology) in all the places Frost claims. It seems better to put forward more modest claims.

Let us begin quietly, then, by saying that it is not outrageous to regard Daniel as an apocalyptic work. Some would prefer to insert some qualifications even into this statement,

[1] S. B. Frost, *Old Testament Apocalyptic*, p. 113.
[2] *Ibid.*, p. 120.

but I am here doing no more than point to a generally held assessment. Indeed it is often held that Daniel was the first apocalypse and that its popularity brought imitators and in due time the appearance of a new literary genre. Sometimes there is an explicit connection of later apocalyptic with Daniel as when the author of 2 *Esdras* writes, 'This is the interpretation of this vision which you have seen: The eagle which you saw coming up from the sea is the fourth kingdom which appeared in a vision to your brother Daniel. But it was not explained to him as I now explain or have explained it to you' (2 *Esdras* 12:10–12).

Apocalyptic is often seen also in passages such as Isaiah 24–27, Ezekiel 38–39, the prophecy of Joel and Zechariah 9–14. Others are sometimes cited, but these seem the principal places. We proceed to discuss them briefly.

The book of Daniel

H. H. Rowley lays it down that 'the Book of Daniel is the first great apocalyptic work', and cites Bousset-Gressmann in support, 'With Daniel begins the apocalyptic literature of Judaism.'[3] Such views are widely held and it is not uncommon to find it affirmed that it was the great success that attended this writing that led to the class of apocalyptic. This is not to deny that there was foreign as well as Hebrew influence on apocalyptic, nor that sometimes writing not unlike Jewish apocalyptic may be found in other literatures. Everyone agrees that apocalyptic drew from many sources. But the idea is that in Daniel for the first time on Jewish soil at least, and probably for the first time anywhere, the diverse elements that go to make up apocalyptic were successfully put together in a book which had wide appeal.

Much in Daniel is, of course, not apocalyptic. The inspiring stories in the opening chapters with their examples of noble courage in the service of God do not come under this heading. It is suggested that there were such stories in circulation, mostly centring on the exploits of an ancient worthy

[3] H. H. Rowley, *The Relevance of Apocalyptic*, p. 43 and n. 4.

named Daniel, but including also some other young men of courage and faith. These were eminently suited to encouraging the faithful in times of special difficulty and persecution, as for example during the Maccabean troubles. Someone alert to the needs of the times gathered these stories together and made them an introduction to his own message. This he conveyed not in further Daniel-type stories, but in a series of visions which he ascribed to Daniel. His aim was not to write history but to hearten God's people in difficult days with a 'tract for the times'.

In this second section of the book there is a continuing use of symbolism featuring a variety of curious animals often with unusual numbers of horns. The use of numbers is also significant, as is that of mysterious expressions such as 'a time, times, and half a time'. Throughout there is the thought that God is supreme and that in due time He will overthrow the evil. Until that day it seems that all that the righteous can do is put up with the evil, for they cannot overthrow it themselves. This is characteristic of apocalyptic and we have already noticed that ideas such as these are found again and again in apocalyptic literature.

So far it seems that, apart from the opening chapters, Daniel is a work of apocalyptic. But there are some problems. In the first place there is the question of authorship. Apocalypses are mostly fathered on to great names from the past. Those who regard Daniel as a typical apocalypse claim that this has been done here. The author has ascribed his book to a hero of Babylonian times. Unfortunately for this view, however, we know nothing of such a Daniel. The name does not occur again in the Old Testament, though the very similar name Dan'el is found in Ezekiel 14:14, 20; 28:3. Quite apart from the slight difference in the name, Ezekiel's Dan'el is linked with Noah and Job in chapter 14 and with 'the prince of Tyre' in chapter 28. Neither connects him with sixth-century Babylon. The name is found also in the Ras Shamra tablets, again in the form Dan'el,[4] where the reference is to a mythical character described as the 'Dispenser of Fertility'.

---

[4] See *Documents from Old Testament Times*, ed. D. Winton Thomas, London, 1958, pp. 124ff.

D

As the date is 1400 BC we are again far removed from the
leading figure of the book of Daniel. Many discount the
difference in the names and hold that our book of Daniel
is referring to the same being as are Ezekiel and/or the Ras
Shamra tablets. But in the first place there seems no good
reason for our overlooking the difference in the names, and
in the second, even if the same man is in mind, these passages
add nothing to our knowledge of him. They certainly do
not prove that he was a folk hero or the like. Nothing connects him with Babylon or with the sixth century BC. When
all is said, the fact remains that 'Daniel' appears only in
the book bearing his name. Nothing can be added except a
few references to the similar sounding 'Dan'el'. It cannot be
said that the case for an ancient hero named Daniel has
been convincingly made out. To urge that Daniel, though
unknown to us outside this book, was well known in Old
Testament times is to bolster up one hypothesis with
another.[5]

Another possibility is to take up Rowley's position, that the
book is written round the Daniel stories. When he has re-
counted these tales of heroic endeavour, this view holds, the
author proceeded to add his visions in Daniel's name, 'not
in order to deceive his readers, but in order to reveal his
identity with the author of the Daniel stories'.[6] But when
later writers of this kind of book saw Daniel as pseudonymous
they copied this feature and it thus became part of the normal
apocalyptic method. But even if this be accepted (and some
hold that other pieces of apocalyptic such as Is. 24–27 are
earlier) the method used in this book is different from that
pursued so consistently by the apocalyptists in general.

Again, we have noted that there is a difference between
prophecy and apocalyptic, even if the difference is at times
difficult to define with precision. On one occasion, at any

[5] H. H. Rowley rejects Russell's view that apocalyptic pseudonymity
represents 'extensions of the personality' of those whose names were
used, saying, *inter alia*, 'For no possible reason could be suggested for
the author of Daniel's selection of Daniel as the name under which to
write, since a Daniel of the sixth century BC at the court of Nebuchad-
nezzar is otherwise quite unknown, and he had no known personality
to "extend" until this book was written' (*op. cit.*, p. 41, n. 1).
[6] H. H. Rowley, *op. cit.*, p. 40.

rate, the author classes this work (or part of it) as coming within the orbit of the prophet (Dn. 9:24). But as the same verse speaks of sealing up the vision, a characteristic apocalyptic concept, the point has little value. Whether the book should be classed as prophecy or apocalyptic must be decided on other grounds than this.

Part of our difficulty is that Daniel has affinities with earlier prophecy as well as with later apocalyptic. Thus James A. Montgomery sees this book as 'the connecting hinge' between the canonical writings and apocalyptic.[7] He finds 'little that is otherwise than genuine development of the older Bible religion'[8] which looks like classing the book as a development of prophecy, but he can also say that it 'belongs as a whole to the category of Apocalyptic'.[9] While recognizing that the book has its links with prophecy then Montgomery comes down on the side of apocalyptic.

But quite a number of students take very seriously the remark of Adam C. Welch that 'it may be wiser . . . to interpret Daniel from his predecessors rather than from his successors'.[1] Norman Porteous is one such. Specifically he thinks that this book 'shares with the oracles of the great eighth- and seventh- and sixth-century prophets the view that history has an end which will be brought about by God and that, when that consummation comes, there will be a judgment which will make manifest who are on God's side and who are at enmity with God'.[2] He examines and rejects the view of A. Bentzen and E. W. Heaton that the book should be classed with the Wisdom literature.[3]

Heaton sees it in some ways as 'definitely misleading' to class Daniel with apocalyptic writing.[4] His point is that, while there are undoubted resemblances, if we neglect the very important differences and see Daniel as no more than another piece of apocalyptic we will miss some of the important things

[7] J. A. Montgomery, *A Critical and Exegetical Commentary on the Book of Daniel*, Edinburgh, 1959, p. 78.
[8] *Ibid.*, p. 85.
[9] *Ibid.*, p. 78.
[1] A. C. Welch, *Visions of the End*, p. 129.
[2] N. Porteous, *Daniel*, London, 1965, pp. 14f.
[3] *Ibid.*, pp. 15f.
[4] E. W. Heaton, *The Book of Daniel*, London, 1964, p. 35.

it is saying. He argues that Daniel inherited 'not a formed apocalyptic tradition, but, rather, a miscellaneous body of prophetic teaching and imagery about the coming Kingdom of God'.[5] His contention is that, while a good deal of this miscellaneous matter was taken up into the real apocalypses like *1 Enoch*, the *Sibylline Oracles*, the *Assumption of Moses* and *2 Esdras*, Daniel did not take it up. In fact 'this prophetic material is *almost entirely absent from the Book of Daniel*'.[6] He gives as examples of the kind of thing that is absent from Daniel but found in the apocalypses, cosmic imagery, great battle scenes, 'lurid descriptions of the fate of the wicked gentiles', highly coloured pictures of the final Kingdom and the frequent interest in the Messiah.[7] Heaton sees it as significant that Daniel was accepted into the canon whereas the apocalypses were not and concludes witheringly, 'Daniel has suffered the misfortune of being classed with his second-rate imitators.'[8]

It is thus clear that the book of Daniel is a puzzling one still and it is not clear to which class of literature it should be assigned. No-one can miss its affinity with the apocalypses, but it is to ignore the evidence when it is concluded without further ado that the book is simply an apocalypse. The fact is that it has affinities with the Wisdom literature as well as with apocalyptic, and stronger affinities still with prophecy. There is a lot to be said for Porteous's summary:

> Perhaps the wisest course is to take the Book of Daniel as a distinctive piece of literature with a clearly defined witness of its own, and to take note of the various ways in which it borrows from and is coloured by the earlier prophetic literature, the Wisdom literature and the Psalms and has its successors in the apocalypses, though these often exhibit an extravagance and a fantastic imagination which is less prominent in the Book of Daniel.[9]

We should not miss the uniqueness of this book. It is like the apocalypses it is true, and there can be little doubt that

[5] *Ibid.*, p. 34.
[6] *Ibid.*, Heaton's italics.
[7] *Ibid.*, pp. 34f.
[8] *Ibid.*, p. 37.   [9] N. Porteous, *op. cit.*, p. 16

many of the apocalyptists copied its form. But its essence is otherwise.

Isaiah 24–27

T. H. Robinson wrote of Isaiah 24–27 as 'a great Apocalypse', and again as, apart from Daniel, 'the most characteristic piece of Apocalypse in the Old Testament'.[1] He lists the factors that bring him to this verdict: 'the violent interference of Yahweh in the world, His "supernatural" methods, His triumphant destruction of His foes, the universal outlook, the salvation of Israel from distress and her ultimate supremacy.'[2] George A. F. Knight is another who clearly regards these chapters as apocalyptic, for he heads his treatment of them 'The "Little Apocalypse" ' without thinking it necessary to demonstrate the point.[3] His quote marks indicate that some qualification is intended, but his discussion casts no doubt on the classification.

But some hesitation is in order. These chapters share some of the characteristics of apocalyptic. For example they speak of world-wide judgment[4] and they view the intervention of God on the last great day as the one way in which the evil the author sees at work in the world will be overcome. But, while this is not unlike apocalyptic, it falls short of being the

[1] T. H. Robinson, *Prophecy and the Prophets in Ancient Israel*, London, 1941, pp. 93, 202.

[2] *Ibid.*, p. 202.

[3] G. A. F. Knight, *Prophets of Israel (1) Isaiah* (*Bible Guides*, ed. William Barclay and F. F. Bruce), London, 1961, pp. 37, 84. In the former passage he does speak of the 'so-called "Little Apocalypse" in chs. 24–27'. S. B. Frost should also be mentioned. He finds that in these chapters apocalyptic 'first achieves its characteristic form' (*Old Testament Apocalyptic*, p. 143).

[4] *Cf.* George Buchanan Gray, 'in chs. 1–23 we have in the forefront the particular circumstances or fates of definite and particular nations – Jewish or foreign, in chs. 24–27 the future both of judgment and of promise that awaits the world at large. We pass from prophecy to apocalypse' (*A Critical and Exegetical Commentary on the Book of Isaiah I–XXXIX*, Edinburgh, 1912, p. 397; he can also use a heading over his translation of most of this section, 'An Apocalyptic Poem', p. 404). But this is to take one feature and make it the decisive criterion of apocalyptic.

genuine article. It is eschatology indeed, but apocalyptic is not
to be identified with eschatology. Here there is, for example,
none of the curious symbolism so beloved of the apocalyptists,
no dualism or division of time into periods or the doctrine
of the two ages. Long ago J. Skinner commented on both the
likeness to apocalyptic and the fundamental dissimilarity:
'the strongly-marked apocalyptic character of the ideas and
imagery has impressed nearly all commentators. There has
perhaps been a tendency to exaggerate this feature; if we
compare the passage with a typical apocalypse, like the book
of Daniel, the differences are certainly more striking than the
resemblances.'[5]

It is best to recognize that apocalyptic did not suddenly
burst on the scene, fully developed and perfect in all its parts.
There were foreshadowings and beginnings. Ideas and
imagery appeared in diverse places and were combined.
There was growth and progress. Passages like these Isaianic
chapters show the kind of thinking that was capable of
developing and in due course did develop into apocalyptic.
But it is premature to see it in this place.

Other Old Testament passages

Fairly similar comments may be made about other passages
from the Old Testament. Several are claimed as apocalyptic
but it will usually be seen that, while they have some of the
characteristics of this genre, they lack others. We should see
them as forming part of the background to apocalyptic and
as showing the kind of outlook that in due time would lead
to apocalyptic. But they do not themselves form part of that
genre.

As an example, some point to Ezekiel 38–39, chapters
which feature the activities and final overthrow of Gog of
the land of Magog.[6] Montgomery says of this and chapters

---

[5] J. Skinner, *The Book of the Prophet Isaiah, chapters I–XXXIX*,
Cambridge, 1900, p. 179.
[6] For a discussion of the significance of these figures and references to the
literature see H. H. Rowley, *The Relevance of Apocalyptic*, pp. 35ff.

47f., 'Ezekiel has a full-blown Apocalyptic'.[7] Similarly G. A. Cooke heads his discussion of these two chapters simply 'An Apocalypse, chs. 38, 39'.[8] Gog and Magog undoubtedly are symbolic names and the forces of evil they represent are familiar in apocalyptic. There is also the thought of the overwhelming might of evil against which normal human forces are of no avail. But in the end it is God who intervenes and subdues them. This is not unlike apocalyptic, but of itself it scarcely merits the description. It is better, with S. B. Frost, to say, 'Ezekiel has laid the ground-plan of apocalyptic'.[9]

It is much the same with the book of Joel[1] or with Zechariah 9–14. The Day of the Lord figures largely in the thinking of the authors of such passages. There is also an emphasis on the terror the final intervention of the Lord would create when He came to destroy all evil. The Zechariah chapters also bring us something very like the miseries that would precede the coming of the Messianic age.[2] All this marks an emphasis on eschatology, but, as we have already noticed, apocalyptic is more than eschatology. However difficult it may be to define, it yet has a number of other characteristics, as I have tried to show in the preceding pages. But such prophecies as Joel and Zechariah lack far too many of them to be considered as examples of this literary genre. What they do is to show that there was a long history behind the kind of thinking that would ultimately issue in apocalyptic and that this kind of literature developed by degrees. Before it emerged as a recognizable literary genre there were many writings embodying one or other of the characteristics that ultimately were to come together and make up the apocalyptic we have been concerned with in this book.

[7] J. A. Montgomery, *A Critical and Exegetical Commentary on the Book of Daniel*, p. 79.
[8] G. A. Cooke, *A Critical and Exegetical Commentary on the Book of Ezekiel*, Edinburgh, 1936, p. 406. John B. Taylor refers to the passage as 'an apocalyptic oracle' (*Ezekiel*, London, 1969, p. 241).
[9] S. B. Frost, *Old Testament Apocalyptic*, p. 92.
[1] Frost sees the last part of this book as apocalyptic (*op. cit.*, ch. 9).
[2] T. H. Robinson finds 'nothing that can strictly be called apocalyptic' in Zechariah 9–11, but in chs. 12–14 'the apocalyptic thought and language are unmistakable' (*Prophecy and the Prophets in Ancient Israel*, p. 205).

Part of our problem may be that there is no such thing as 'a typical apocalypse', so that it is not clear beyond all argument when the genre has finally made its appearance. Many scholars, as we have seen, hold that enough of the characteristics of apocalyptic are found in some at any rate of the passages we have been examining to justify the use of the term, apocalyptic. Others are hesitant.

Perhaps it would not be unfair to see in these prophecies an expression of the thought that the world is moving towards a new era when Yahweh would bring history to a close. Men would be judged and the Golden Age would come. All this would be given emphasis and precision and would be expressed in characteristic symbolism by the apocalyptic writers. Undoubtedly in these passages we are moving towards apocalyptic, feeling out after it, if you like.[3] But there is good reason for holding that we have not reached it yet.

[3] John Mauchline, commenting on Isaiah 24–27, says, 'it is possible to discern in the transition from chs. 1–23 to chs. 24–27 how prophecy, with its distinctive characteristics, could pass easily and by imperceptible degrees into apocalyptic' (*Isaiah 1–39*, London, 1962, p. 183). He does not appear to mean that chs. 24–27 are in fact apocalyptic, for he speaks of them only as 'having some of the characteristics of apocalyptic literature' (*ibid.*).

APOCALYPTIC AND
THE NEW TESTAMENT

It is often said there is a good deal of apocalyptic in the New Testament. The two principal places where this is to be seen are Mark 13 and the book of Revelation. But other passages are thought to be of the same essential kind, especially 1 Corinthians 15 and 2 Thessalonians 2. It is not, however, simply a matter of citing this book or that. As we saw in the opening section of this study, there are those who see most of the essential concepts and thought forms of Christianity as deriving from an apocalyptic milieu. The thought is that apocalyptic represents that part of Judaism which did not emphasize the Law as did orthodox Rabbinism and that it was from this sector of Judaism that Christianity developed.

There is truth here, as we saw earlier. There is every reason for holding that Christianity developed from the 'enthusiastic' side of Judaism rather than from the formal side represented by the Pharisees and, from a somewhat different point of view, the Sadducees. But it must not be overlooked that there were other strands in Judaism also. There were the Zealots and the Herodians and others. In recent years the Qumran scrolls have given us a glimpse of one of these communities from the inside. Whether we identify the Qumran sect with the Essenes or not is not important for our present purpose. They were distinctively different from the orthodoxy of the day and they underline the fact that first-century Judaism was far from being monolithic. The evidence shows that there were great diversities of opinion and practice. That apocalyptic contributed something to Christianity is plain enough, but that it stood to the new faith in the relation of parent to child is going too far.

Long ago Sanday expressed a more balanced opinion. He

saw the influence of apocalyptic in much of the terminology
of the Gospels, but saw also a connection with prophecy:

> Looking at the contents of the Gospels broadly, we are
> struck by the fact that so many of the leading terms
> employed in them should be either directly apocalyptic or
> closely associated with apocalyptism. This is true of the
> whole group of titles of which our Lord Himself and the
> Primitive Church made use to describe His mission: such
> titles as Messiah, Son of David, Son of man, Son of God.
> And it is no less true of another group of prominent terms
> which describe the aim and effect of His mission in its
> working among men – kingdom of God (or of heaven),
> repentance, judgment, watchfulness, resurrection. All these
> terms, if not exactly apocalyptic in origin – for many of
> them go back to the earlier period of prophecy – had
> acquired an almost technical sense in the apocalyptic
> vocabulary.[1]

This, I think, must be accepted. The Christian movement
has its affinities with the apocalyptic movement. The language of the apocalyptists has influenced that of the Christians.
The characteristic expressions of the Gospels often seem to
receive more emphasis in apocalyptic than they do, for
example, in the Old Testament.

This is being emphasized by many New Testament scholars
who are impressed by the place eschatology occupies in the
New Testament writings generally and by the consciousness
of the early Christians that they were led by the Spirit of God.
G. Ebeling, while he rejects many of E. Käsemann's contentions, yet agrees that 'the basic conception is correct; the
primitive Christian proclamation is characterized from the
start by eschatological near expectation and by prophetic
workings of the Spirit'.[2]

But he also reminds us that there are important differences
between the apocalypses and the New Testament. In the
latter we have

[1] W. Sanday, in *The Hibbert Journal*, x, 1911–12, p. 96.
[2] G. Ebeling, in *Journal for Theology and the Church*, no. 6, 1969, p. 49.

... not apocalyptic systems of ideas, but individual sayings with an apocalyptic background; not a disclosure of apocalyptic mysteries, but concrete, apocalyptically grounded instructions for the present, not a code language of dreams and visions, but one that is universally understandable, not a prophetic authority that is borrowed under a pseudonym, but one that is exercised in personal responsibility.[3]

These differences are important. It is one thing to see Christianity as indebted to the apocalyptists for some of its ideas and expressions. But it is quite another to see the apocalyptic movement as largely responsible for the appearance of Christianity or to see the New Testament writings as essentially apocalyptic in character. The evidence simply does not bear out such contentions. We proceed to look in greater detail at the two places where the influence of apocalyptic is held to be most obvious, namely, Mark 13 and the book of Revelation.

Mark 13

Mark 13 is often claimed with especial confidence as a specimen of Jewish apocalyptic. The 'Little Apocalypse' theory, indeed, sees a considerable part of this chapter as an authentic Jewish writing. Those who put the theory forward maintain that an earlier Jewish apocalypse has been combined with more specifically Christian material to produce the result that is before us.[4] Sanday cannot be described as a strong supporter of the theory (he remains uncertain whether the verses in question should be regarded as an interpolation or not), but he puts the essence of it clearly. The verses in question

fall easily into a sort of drama in three acts, describing the final catastrophe in the familiar language of Jewish apocalyptic: first the so-called 'woes' or 'travail-pangs of the Messiah', the famines and wars and rumours of wars which

[3] *Ibid.*, pp. 52f.
[4] See, for example, R. Bultmann, *The History of the Synoptic Tradition*, Oxford, 1963, p. 122; V. Taylor, *The Gospel according to St. Mark*, London, 1959, pp. 498ff.

were to be the preliminary signs of the approaching end; then, the gradual culmination of horrors, 'the abomination of desolation in the holy place', vaguely hinted at in prophecy; and, lastly, the appearance of the Son of man on the clouds of heaven. The lurid colouring of this picture is all strictly Jewish.[5]

It cannot be doubted that there are some striking resemblances to the typical Jewish apocalypse in these verses. Even those who reject the 'Little Apocalypse' theory most firmly can scarcely deny this. Whatever the origin of these words they have certainly been influenced by the vocabulary of apocalyptic.

Yet it would not be right to let the matter rest there. If there are real resemblances there are also real differences. Some of the most characteristic features of this chapter are not to be found in apocalyptic. In the words of C. E. B. Cranfield,

> . . . this discourse differs radically from typical Jewish apocalyptic. While the language of apocalyptic is indeed used, the purpose for which it is used and even the form of the discourse are different. While it is characteristic of Jewish apocalypses that the seer is himself addressed or else relates in the first person what he has seen and heard, this discourse is marked throughout by its use of the second person plural imperative. It is in fact exhortation, not ordinary apocalyptic. Its purpose is not to impart esoteric information but to sustain faith and obedience.[6]

Long ago Wellhausen made much the same point, saying, 'It belongs to the form of real Jewish apocalypses that *the Seer himself* is addressed, whether by God, or an angel of God, or that he recounts with an "I" what he has been permitted to see and hear.'[7] G. R. Beasley-Murray cites this passage and immediately goes on,

[5] W. Sanday, in *The Hibbert Journal*, x, 1911–12, pp. 94f.
[6] C. E. B. Cranfield, *The Gospel according to Saint Mark*, Cambridge, 1959, p. 388.
[7] Cited by G. R. Beasley-Murray, in *The Expository Times*, lxiv, 1952–53, pp. 348f.

This 'un-Jewish' element is not confined to a few sayings in the discourse, it is consistently maintained throughout its length. Its first word is an imperative, *Watch* (*v.* 5), and its last is a synonym of that, also in the imperative; between them no fewer than sixteen imperatives are scattered. It is doubtful if any apocalypse could be adduced in which teaching and exhortation are so competely mixed.[8]

The fact must be faced that in this chapter we have an urgent exhortation to true discipleship rather than a typical specimen of apocalyptic speculation. There is much about the last things, it is true. But the emphasis is not there. The emphasis is on a true and loyal following of Jesus, on being faithful disciples no matter what the the trials.

And it is not only the main thrust. While there is undoubted use of conventional apocalyptic language, it is also the case that much that is normal in contemporary apocalyptic is absent. Joachim Jeremias has drawn attention to this. He is concerned to find the authentic teaching of Jesus and he agrees that in Mark 13 there is a good deal of use of 'traditional apocalyptic themes'. He finds this 'to a greater extent than is the case elsewhere in the sayings of Jesus'. But before accepting this as another piece of apocalyptic he has more to say. He goes on to notice important differences from apocalyptic.

> Nevertheless, it would be uncritical if we were to overlook the fact that Mark 13 differs fundamentally from contemporary apocalyptic in that decisive themes of the apocalyptic of the time are absent: the holy war, the annihilation of Rome, the feelings of hate and vengeance, the gathering of the Diaspora, the sensual, earthly portrayal of salvation, the renewal of Jerusalem as the capital of a mighty realm, rule over the Gentiles, the luxuriance of life in the new age, etc. None of this is to be found in Mark 13.[9]

To this list we might add the last judgment, the overthrow of Satan and the destruction of evil, all themes we might expect

[8] *Ibid.*, p. 349.
[9] J. Jeremias, *New Testament Theology*, Part One, London, 1971, pp. 124f.

in an apocalypse. Not only are important apocalyptic themes
absent from this chapter, but there are some discordant notes.
Thus there is the thought that Israel herself will be hurt by
the catastrophe, and particularly that the temple will suffer.
Jewish apocalyptic expected that the nation would triumph
or at any rate that part of it which constituted the true Israel.
And the temple was seen as especially under the protection of
God. All this makes it impossible to see Mark 13 as just
another apocalypse. There are differences which are as
important as the resemblances.

Charles B. Cousar in fact sees an anti-apocalyptic thrust in
this chapter. Mark, he thinks, is directing 'the attention of
the community away from a preoccupation with apocalyptic
calculations to an immediate and urgent discipleship'.[1] Later
he refers to the chapter as 'a speech in which he has opposed
apocalyptic speculation'.[2]

The point should be clear. That the language of this chapter has been influenced by that of the apocalypses seems beyond doubt. That this is simply another apocalypse is another
thing again. What we have here is a phenomenon that recurs
throughout the New Testament. Clearly Jesus was not
unacquainted with apocalyptic terminology and ideas. But
equally clearly He was not simply a representative of apocalypticism. This may be said also of the New Testament writers
generally. Whatever apocalyptic terms they may borrow they
are not apocalyptists. There is a distinctive Christian standpoint.

We see this in another area in the case of the Qumran
scrolls. While there are arresting coincidences of language
and even now and then of ideas between the New Testament
and the scrolls, the essential positions taken up by the New

---

[1] C. B. Cousar, in *Interpretation*, xxiv, 1970, p. 328.

[2] *Ibid.*, p. 333. His position is expressed more fully in this way: 'The
first category of warnings we noted in Mark 13 indicated that the
Evangelist was alerting the Christian community to the dangers of being
caught up in an apocalyptic enthusiasm which expected a near end of
the world. In developing his polemic against such a position, Mark in
effect has taken apocalyptic material being used to arouse speculation
and perhaps excitement, has historicized that material in terms of
present-day events so as to remove their apocalyptic character, and then
has put a brake on the entire process' (*ibid.*, p. 326).

Testament writers and the men of Qumran are poles apart.[3] So with apocalyptic. No thinking Jew of the first century could have been unaware of the general thrust of apocalyptic. Some of its language and some of its ideas were congenial to the Christians and were incorporated in their writings. But that does not make these writings specimens of apocalyptic. Specifically, the form and language of Mark 13 are not such as to enable us to see in it a typical apocalypse. There are highly significant differences as well as resemblances. There is much more to Christianity than apocalyptic.

The Revelation to John

Before we leave this aspect of our subject we must give attention to the last book of the New Testament, for Revelation above all others is confidently hailed as a typical example of apocalyptic. It is commonly called 'the Apocalypse', and indeed we derive the very term 'apocalypse' from the Greek word *apokalypsis* used to describe this book in its opening verse.

Undoubtedly there is much to support this common classification, for apocalyptic characteristics are to be observed throughout the book. Especially is this the case with its symbolism. The modern reader finds himself in trouble with this symbolism again and again. To him it is a totally unfamiliar world. Indeed it is probably this as much as anything that accounts for the comparative neglect of the book throughout modern Christendom. But it was the world in which the apocalyptist was at home. Again, Revelation is like the apocalypses in its eager anticipation of the setting up of God's kingdom and its expectation of a new heaven and a new earth. In this category too we should place its emphasis on angels, and on revelations made through such heavenly beings. In all this, Revelation conforms to the typical apocalyptic canons.

But we should not overlook the fact that there are some

---

[3] I have examined the point, with reference to John's Gospel, in my *Studies in the Fourth Gospel*, Exeter, 1969, ch. 6.

important differences also.[4] To begin with, our writer calls his book a prophecy and that not once but repeatedly (1:3; 22:7, 10, 18, 19). We noticed earlier that it is not easy to differentiate apocalyptic from prophecy, and there are sections in some of the prophetical books that critics usually describe as apocalyptic. But while the precise differentiation of prophecy from apocalyptic is not easy, it can scarcely be denied that a broad distinction may be made between the two. No-one, surely, will contend that prophecy and apocalyptic are synonymous terms. It is then significant that our author specifically classes his book with the prophets. In line with this is the fact that his visions convey the word of God (Rev. 1:2).

We have also seen that the prophets usually have a more stringent demand for repentance from those who call themselves God's people than do the apocalyptists. The concern of the latter is rather the comforting of the Lord's own. In this respect Revelation probably has a foot in both camps. On the one hand there is a strong insistence on the importance of upright living. Typical is the series of letters to the seven churches in chapters 2 and 3, where there are stern demands for repentance (2:5, 16, 21, 22; 3:3, 19). There is no glossing over of the offences of Christians. On the other hand, it is just as clear that this book is meant to give comfort and encouragement to the people of God. They were oppressed and fearful, and the Seer takes them behind the scenes so that they may see how God's purposes work out. It is typical of apocalyptic that it looks for the End, and this is the case with this book. God's people are exhorted to hold fast, for God's purpose is being worked out and it will become clear at the End. On this score it would seem that Revelation is partly with the prophets and partly with the apocalypses.

Yet we should notice a difference even in the way John looks for the End. We have noted that the apocalyptists were normally very pessimistic about this age. But John does not see this present world as completely dominated by evil,

[4] *Cf.* A. Oepke, '[Revelation] has many affinities with the literature to which we now refer [*i.e.* apocalyptic], though it cannot be simply classified with it' (*Theological Dictionary of the New Testament*, iii, p. 578).

though he does look for an outbreak of Satanic activity at the last time. For him history is the sphere in which God has wrought out redemption. The really critical thing in the history of mankind has already taken place, and it took place here, on this earth, in the affairs of men. The Lamb 'as it had been slain' dominates the entire book. John sees Christ as victorious and as having won the victory through His death, an event in history. His people share in His triumph, but they have conquered Satan 'by the blood of the Lamb and by the word of their testimony' (Rev. 12:11). The pessimism which defers God's saving activity until the End is absent. Though John depicts evil realistically, his book is fundamentally optimistic.

There are other differences. Thus the apocalypses are normally pseudonymous, but John writes in his own name (Rev. 1:1, 4, 9; 22:8). He does not look for an illustrious predecessor. And if it be objected that John was the name of one of the greatest of our Lord's apostles, the answer must be that the author of this book makes no attempt to indicate that it is that John and not another that is in mind. He says nothing at all about being an apostle. While it is open to any student to argue or assume that the two are identical, the point is that our author makes no claim equivalent to those in the apocalyptic writings.

Bruce W. Jones makes a good deal of this point. He insists that pseudonymity is characteristic of apocalyptic and that this is important. It gives the apocalypses their aura as emanating from the remote past. He sees the function of pseudonymity as simply identifying these books as old ones. It serves a different function from that in other books:

> In apocalyptic, the pseudonym links the present and the past in a particular way; the past is important only because it points to the present. Along with *vaticinium ex eventu* prophecy, pseudonymity says, in effect, 'Now is the decisive time. Even the ancient heroes were talking about us.' Appeal to the past heightens the significance of the present.[5]

[5] B. W. Jones, in *Journal of Biblical Literature*, lxxxvii, 1968, p. 326.

It may be that there is something of an exaggeration here. As we have seen, there is much more to apocalyptic than the voice from the past. But at least it is clear that the appeal to the remote past is a not unimportant feature of apocalyptic, and in this respect the Revelation is different.

Again, the apocalyptists characteristically retrace history, but do so in the guise of prophecy. From the standpoint of someone in the remote past they foretell what will happen up to their own day. Or if they do not do that, at least they speak from the standpoint of the ancient worthy in whose name they write. There is no trace of this in Revelation. Rather, in the manner of the true prophet John takes his stand firmly in his own day and looks resolutely to the future.

G. E. Ladd makes an important point when he sees Revelation as a book which

> embodies the prophetic tension between history and eschatology. The beast is Rome and at the same time an eschatological Antichrist which cannot be fully equated with historical Rome. While the churches of Asia were facing persecution, there is no known persecution in the first century AD which fits that portrayed in the Apocalypse. The shadow of historical Rome is so outlined against the darker shadow of the eschatological Antichrist that it is difficult if not impossible to distinguish between the two. History is eschatologically interpreted; evil at the hands of Rome is realized eschatology.[6]

This kind of tension is seen in the prophets as they addressed themselves to the needs of their own day but looked eagerly for the eschatological 'Day of the Lord'. But we do not see the same thing in the apocalypses.

With Revelation, then, as with Mark 13, there must be caution before we class it with the apocalypses. There are undoubted resemblances and it would be impossible to hold that our author is not indebted to the apocalyptic method. Clearly he knows this kind of writing and glories in it. But equally clearly he has not set himself to write just another apocalypse. His book has its own distinctives. While it has

6 G. E. Ladd, in *Baker's Dictionary of Theology*, p. 53.

connections with apocalyptic it is yet different. It is a Christian writing setting forth what God has done in Christ and what He will yet do, and using something of the apocalyptic method to bring all this out. But the emphasis on 'the Lamb as it had been slain', *i.e.* on a past event of history, is both central to Revelation and absent from the apocalypses.[7]

---

[7] James Kallas has argued that Revelation is not an apocalyptic book because it has an attitude to suffering different from that of the apocalypses ('The Apocalypse – an Apocalyptic Book?' in *Journal of Biblical Literature*, lxxxvi, 1967, pp. 69–80). He maintains that in the apocalypses suffering comes from forces opposed to God, forces that God will eventually crush. Suffering is simply evil and is to be vigorously opposed. By contrast, in other Jewish writings and in Revelation suffering comes from God and is to be submitted to, not resisted. It is just retribution. There may be something in this, but it must be borne in mind that in Revelation the attitude to suffering is more complex than Kallas allows. The author of the book is suffering at the hands of evil men for his witness to God (Rev. 1:9) and similarly the martyrs met their death because of their faithfulness to God (2:13; 6:9–11). There are thus passages in Revelation that regard suffering as an evil inflicted by the enemies of God, as well as passages which see it as a discipline or punishment sent by a righteous God.

APOCALYPTIC AND THE GOSPEL

The point last noted is one that will bear examination against the background of Christianity as a whole and not simply Revelation. It may be doubted whether apocalyptic is a very good vehicle for the expression of the characteristic Christian message. Christianity puts its emphasis on the cross. At base it is a religion that tells us that in the fullness of the time God in the Person of His Son became man. This is a historical event that took place once, and which is dated at a precise point of time. The Son lived among men and closed His perfect life by dying on a cross for man's salvation. After that came His resurrection and ascension, the latter event bringing to a decisive end the events associated with the incarnation. The story does not end there, for following the Great Commission (Mt. 28:19f.) the followers of Jesus are active in proclaiming the gospel message and must be until the end of time. And it is prophesied that in due course that same Jesus will come again to be the Judge of living and dead and to set up His kingdom. There is the ongoing story and this is not unimportant. But the really central thing for Christians, the 'crucial' thing in the literal sense of the term, is the cross. Christians always must look back to that as the ground of their salvation. It is the cross on which all their hopes rest.

In the apocalyptic literature, on the other hand, the emphasis is always on the last judgment and the events associated with it. Apocalyptic is concerned to show men that, no matter how powerful evil seems to be for the present, it will not ultimately triumph. In due time God will call upon all men to give account of themselves. He will judge all men. He will give the wicked their deserts. He will reward the righteous and take them to be with Himself.

The emphasis in the two classes of literature is different.

The apocalypses abandon this world and look forward to the day when God will set up His kingdom. The New Testament writings do not lose sight of this important truth, but they put the critical point, the very centre of things, earlier. This is reserved for what Christ did for our salvation.

F. C. Burkitt brings out the point by referring us to the early Christian apocalypse, *The Ascension of Isaiah*. He points out that this writing makes an unsatisfactory impression on the reader because it tries to do two things at once. He says:

> . . . in the *Ascension of Isaiah* the idea that the End is the chief thing in history is crossed by the new Christian idea that it is the Incarnation of the Messiah, an event now passed, which is the chief thing in history. This new Christian idea, that began with S. Paul and attained more and more fixity and definiteness as time went on, is really fatal to great apocalyptic writing. The Incarnation, the career of Jesus Christ, may be the most important fact in all history past or future; but if so, an Apocalypse is not the proper literary form in which to set it forth.[1]

We cannot have it both ways. Granted that both the incarnation and the End are important, both cannot be the really significant thing. For the apocalypses there is the concentration on the future. In Christianity there is the recognition that the incarnation, with the atonement as its high point, is the most important event of all time. That is why, as Burkitt puts it, an apocalypse is not the proper literary form for setting forth the essential Christian message. The Christians might indeed borrow some of the apocalyptic terminology and approach. Some of their faith could well be tellingly expressed in this way. But the characteristic Christian writing must be the gospel. Ebeling says with emphasis: *'It is no accident that the characteristic literary form of Christianity was the gospel and not the apocalypse.'*[2] This is the heart of the matter. It is the gospel that sets forth the great saving

[1] F. C. Burkitt, *Jewish and Christian Apocalypses*, p. 47.
[2] G. Ebeling, in *Journal for Theology and the Church*, no. 6, 1969, p. 53 (Ebeling's italics).

truth of what God has done for mankind. It must be insisted upon that, if the New Testament is at all reliable, the early church stressed the crucifixion and the resurrection. Its message was that the Saviour had come and had died and risen again. Those who hold that the primitive preaching centres on eschatology are confronted with the awkward fact that this picture cannot be derived from the sources. The early Christians concentrated on the gospel, the message of what God in Christ had done for man's salvation. They were not unmindful, of course, of the future. They looked for the Christ to come as Judge. But even then they did not forget the cross. It was the same Christ that had been crucified who would be the Judge, and it was He whom they preached (*cf.* 1 Cor. 1:23).[3]

It was not only the way of forgiveness that differentiated the Christians from the apocalyptists, but the fact that there should be forgiveness at all. In the New Testament sin looms always as a problem, in fact as *the* problem. It is sin that separates man from God and which must be overcome if man is to be saved. Through all the disputes the theologians have had over the way the atonement is to be understood there has never been any doubt that in some way Jesus did accomplish atonement. Forgiveness is available. Men may now turn away from their sin and find their forgiveness and their peace in God. It is a grand gospel to preach to guilty men.

But the apocalyptists were not proclaiming a gospel. Their only interest in guilty men was that they should be punished. They divided all mankind into the good and the bad. The good, they thought, God would vindicate and deliver from the oppression of their enemies. The bad He would overthrow and utterly destroy. There was no place for repentant sinners in such a scheme. As C. Ryder Smith put it, in apocalyptic 'There is no doctrine of the salvation of sinners, no idea that God would find a way by which bad men might become good . . . the dominant idea was that God will save

---

[3] *Cf.* E. Fuchs, the primitive Jewish-Christian church 'expected as the divine judge one who had been crucified. (And what would there have been for it to proclaim, if it had cherished its expectation in secret?)' (*Journal for Theology and the Church*, no. 6, 1969, p. 72).

good men from trouble, not that He will save bad men from sin'.[4] This difference in emphasis must always be kept in mind when the relationship of Christianity to apocalyptic is being considered. In their attitude to sinners they are saying two very different, even contradictory things. Apocalyptic is not a fit vehicle for conveying the truth about forgiveness.

Nor is it really useful for helping men see the Christian attitude to this world in which we live. The men of the New Testament were convinced that God had broken into this world in the coming of Jesus. As we have already noticed, this has consequences in terms of forgiveness and salvation. But it also has consequences in terms of how we should regard this world. Many writers have spoken of Christianity as world-affirming, and this points us to an important truth. It is a faith that looks to God to act in the here and now. And it looks to its adherents to seek to realize God's will in the here and now. A meek resignation of this world to the powers of evil is never a part of Christianity. The apocalyptists were sure of the ultimate triumph of God and in this they are at one with the Christians. But they surrendered this world to the powers of evil and saw no hope for it. In this their world-view is out of harmony with that of the Christians and there is no way of bringing them together. One of the most fruitful of modern insights is that which speaks of 'holy worldliness' and sees the duty of the Christian as that of living for God in this world, not simply of awaiting 'pie in the sky'. But there is no way of fitting this into the world-view of the apocalyptists.[5]

Some, to be sure, see a certain compatibility between apocalyptic and the essential Christian message. Thus Käsemann refers to the 'central motif' of post-Easter apocalyptic as 'the hope of the epiphany of the Son of man coming to his

[4] C. Ryder Smith, *The Bible Doctrine of Salvation*, London, 1946, p. 99. S. B. Frost has a similar thought, '. . . the apocalyptists were not faced by this problem of God's mercy because their God was not merciful' (*Old Testament Apocalyptic*, pp. 256f.).
[5] James Robinson speaks of 'the transition from "loss of world", which had its being in the language of apocalypticism transmuted into Gnosticism, into worldliness, which had its being in the Jewish establishment which was succeeded after the fall of Jerusalem by normative Judaism and orthodox Christianity' (*Soli Deo Gloria*, ed. J. McDowell Richards, Richmond, Va., 1968, p. 109).

enthronement'. He goes on, '. . . it is a question whether Christian theology can ever make do, or be legitimate, without this motif which arose from the experience of Easter and determined the Easter faith'.[6] Now it is true to say that the *parousia* with all it means is the necessary outcome of the Easter events. The one inevitably leads on to the other. But to see them as bound up with one another is not the same thing as to see them as equally important. It still remains true that it is not easy to express the centrality of the cross in apocalyptic terms. The *parousia* is important, but it is not the gospel.

We should also bear in mind the fact that most seem agreed that Jesus Himself was not an apocalyptist. Even Käsemann, who puts so much stress on the close connection between apocalyptic and the Christian message, indeed who sees them as in some sense one, agrees that this was not Jesus' teaching He thinks that Jesus stressed the nearness of God, and that apocalyptic was the early church's response to His teaching. This does but deepen the mystery. If Jesus was not basically an apocalyptist, why should the response to His teaching take this form? It is much better to see apocalyptic as but one strand in the church's message. It expresses some things well, particularly the eager looking forward to the End.

But apocalyptic is not a good medium for expressing 'the cruciality of the cross' and in fact it does not express it. Where the New Testament writers are concerned with the last things and final judgment they can use apocalyptic vividly and forcefully. But where they deal with Christ's saving work they use categories like justification by faith, reconciliation, the new covenant sealed with Christ's blood, and others. Here apocalyptic is not helpful. The New Testament writers do not use it and we can see why. Apocalyptic is simply not suitable as a way of bringing out such truths. And since Christ's atoning work is the central doctrine of New Testament Christianity, apocalyptic fails us at the heart of the faith.

In other words, we must accept apocalyptic as part of the background of the New Testament message. We cannot

[6] E. Käsemann, in *Journal for Theology and the Church*, no. 6, 1969, p. 46.

understand important sections of the New Testament without some knowledge of apocalyptic. But we cannot hold that apocalyptic contains the key to the whole. It cannot express the great central doctrine of the faith. It is not well adapted to expressing the heart of the faith. At base Christianity is the gospel. And 'gospel' is not an apocalyptic term.

BIBLIOGRAPHY

(This is not a reading list, but is confined to books and articles to which reference has in fact been made in the text or footnotes.)

C. K. Barrett, *The New Testament Background: Selected Documents*, London, 1957.

W. A. Beardslee, 'New Testament Apocalyptic in Recent Interpretation', in *Interpretation*, xxv, 1971.

G. R. Beasley-Murray, 'The Rise and Fall of the Little Apocalypse Theory', in *The Expository Times*, lxiv, 1952-53.

H. D. Betz, 'On the Problem of the Religio-Historical Understanding of Apocalypticism', in *Journal for Theology and the Church*, no. 6, 1969.

G. H. Box, '4 Ezra', in *The Apocrypha and Pseudepigrapha of the Old Testament*, ed. R. H. Charles, ii, Oxford, 1963.

C. E. Braaten, 'The Significance of Apocalypticism for Systematic Theology', in *Interpretation*, xxv, 1971.

L. H. Brockington, *A Critical Introduction to the Apocrypha*, London, 1961.

—'The Problem of Pseudonymity', in *Journal of Theological Studies*, n.s., iv, 1953.

R. Bultmann, *The History of the Synoptic Tradition*, Oxford, 1963.

F. C. Burkitt, *Jewish and Christian Apocalypses*, London, 1914.

D. R. Catchpole, 'The Problem of the Historicity of the Sanhedrin Trial', in *The Trial of Jesus*, ed. E. Bammel, London, 1970.

R. H. Charles, *The Apocrypha and Pseudepigrapha of the Old Testament*, ii, Oxford, 1963.

R. H. Charles, *Religious Development Between the Old and the New Testaments*, London, 1914.

H. Conzelmann, *An Outline of the Theology of the New Testament*, London, 1969.

G. A. Cooke, *A Critical and Exegetical Commentary on the Book of Ezekiel*, Edinburgh, 1936.

C. B. Cousar, 'Eschatology and Mark's *Theologia Crucis*', in *Interpretation*, xxiv, 1970.

C. E. B. Cranfield, *The Gospel According to St. Mark*, Cambridge, 1959.

F. M. Cross, 'New Directions in the Study of Apocalyptic', in *Journal for Theology and the Church*, no. 6, 1969.

W. D. Davies, *Christian Origins and Judaism*, London, 1962.

— *Paul and Rabbinic Judaism*, London, 1948.

— art. ' Contemporary Jewish Religion', in *Peake's Commentary on the Bible*, ed. M. Black and H. H. Rowley, London, 1962.

G. Ebeling, 'The Ground of Christian Theology', in *Journal for Theology and the Church*, no. 6, 1969.

W. Eichrodt, *Theology of the Old Testament*, ii, London, 1967.

W. Förster, *Palestinian Judaism in New Testament Times*, Edinburgh and London, 1964.

D. N. Freedman, 'The Flowering of Apocalyptic', in *Journal for Theology and the Church*, no. 6, 1969.

S. B. Frost, *Old Testament Apocalyptic*, London, 1952.

E. Fuchs, 'On the Task of a Christian Theology', in *Journal for Theology and the Church*, no. 6, 1969.

R. H. Fuller, *A Critical Introduction to the New Testament*, London, 1966.

G. Gloege, *The Day of His Coming*, London, 1963.

G. B. Gray, *A Critical and Exegetical Commentary on the Book of Isaiah I–XXXIX*, Edinburgh, 1912.

R. G. Hamerton-Kelly, 'The Temple and the Origins of Jewish Apocalyptic', in *Vetus Testamentum*, xx, 1970.

P. D. Hanson, 'Old Testament Apocalyptic Reexamined', in *Interpretation*, xxv, 1971.

J. Hastings, *Dictionary of the Bible*, 2nd ed. rev. F. C. Grant and H. H. Rowley, Edinburgh, 1963.

E. W. Heaton, *The Book of Daniel*, London, 1964.

E. Hennecke, *New Testament Apocrypha*, ed. W. Schneemelcher, trans. R. McL. Wilson, ii, London, 1965.

D. A. Hubbard, art. 'Wisdom Literature', in *The New Bible
Dictionary*, ed. J. D. Douglas *et al.*, London, 1962.

J. Jeremias, *New Testament Theology*, Part One, London,
1971.

B. W. Jones, 'More about the Apocalypse as Apocalyptic', in
Journal of Biblical Literature, lxxxvii, 1968.

J. Kallas, 'The Apocalypse—an Apocalyptic Book?' in
Journal of Biblical Literature, lxxxvi, 1967.

E. Käsemann, 'The Beginnings of Christian Theology',
in *Journal for Theology and the Church*, no. 6,
1969.

G. A. F. Knight, *Prophets of Israel* (1) *Isaiah* (*Bible Guides*,
ed. William Barclay and F. F. Bruce), London, 1961.

J. L. Koole, art. 'Apocalyptic Literature', in *The Encyclopedia of Christianity*, i, ed. Edwin H. Palmer *et al.*,
Wilmington, Delaware, 1964.

G. E. Ladd, art. 'Apocalyptic', in *Baker's Dictionary of
Theology*, Grand Rapids, 1960.

J. Mauchline, *Isaiah 1–39*, London, 1962.

R. Meyer, art. *'prophetes'*, in *Theological Dictionary of the
New Testament*, ed. G. Friedrich, trans. G. W. Bromiley,
vi, Grand Rapids, 1968.

J. A. Montgomery, *A Critical and Exegetical Commentary on
the Book of Daniel*, Edinburgh, 1959.

G. F. Moore, *Judaism*, i, Harvard, 1958.

L. Morris, *Studies in the Fourth Gospel*, Exeter, 1969.

C. F. D. Moule, *The Birth of the New Testament*, London,
1962.

W. R. Murdock, 'History and Revelation in Jewish Apocalypticism', in *Interpretation*, xxi, 1967.

A. Oepke, art. *'kalupto'*, in *Theological Dictionary of the
New Testament*, ed. G. Kittel, trans. G. W. Bromiley, iii,
Grand Rapids, 1965.

N. Porteous, *Daniel*, London, 1965.

J. Robinson, *Soli Deo Gloria*, ed. J. McDowell Richards,
Richmond, Va., 1968.

T. H. Robinson, *Prophecy and the Prophets in Ancient Israel*, London, 1941.

W. G. Rollins, 'The New Testament and Apocalyptic', in *New Testament Studies*, 17, 1970–71.

H. H. Rowley, *The Relevance of Apocalyptic*, London, 1963.

D. S. Russell, *The Method and Message of Jewish Apocalyptic*, London, 1964.

W. Sanday, 'The Apocalyptic Element in the Gospels', in *The Hibbert Journal*, x, 1911–12.

E. Schürer, *A History of the Jewish People in the Time of Jesus Christ*, II, iii, Edinburgh, 1886.

A. Schweitzer, *The Quest of the Historical Jesus*, London, 1945.

E. F. Scott, *The Book of Revelation*, London, 1939.

J. Skinner, *The Book of the Prophet Isaiah, chapters I–XXXIX*, Cambridge, 1900.

C. Ryder Smith, *The Bible Doctrine of Salvation*, London, 1946.

E. Stauffer, *New Testament Theology*, London, 1955.

J. B. Taylor, *Ezekiel*, London, 1969.

V. Taylor, *The Gospel According to St. Mark*, London, 1959.

D. W. Thomas, ed., *Documents from Old Testament Times*, London, 1958.

C. C. Torrey, art. 'Apocalypse', in *The Jewish Encyclopedia*.

P. Vielhauer, 'Apocalypses and Related Subjects – Introduction', in *New Testament Apocrypha*, ii, London, 1965.

E. Voegelin, *Order and History*, vol. i, *Israel and Revelation*, Louisiana, 1969.

G. von Rad, *Old Testament Theology*, ii, London, 1965.

A. C. Welch, *Visions of the End*, London, n.d.

A. N. Wilder, 'The Rhetoric of Ancient and Modern Apocalyptic', in *Interpretation*, xxv, 1971.

P. Winter, *On the Trial of Jesus*, Berlin, 1961.